...•• Contents ••...

Theory

Stick & Quick

Punch Art

Embossing

Stamping

UTEE

Plastics

Introduction

Within these pages you'll find many of the favourite techniques used by cardmakers, alongside new ideas and twists on traditional methods.

The sections are colour-coded, with a selection of techniques within each category. Each section will show you in easy-to-follow steps how to achieve perfect end results. You'll also find accompanying tools lists so you can equip yourself with everything you need before you start. Then to help you apply the techniques, there are plentiful cards that come with full supplies lists and 'how to make' steps. Gain inspiration from these designs and let your imagination run wild!

At the back of the book is a themed gallery for some of the regular occasions for which we would send a greeting. They are great for anybody with cardmaker's block, or for a leisurely flick through with your feet up and a hot cuppa on the go. There's also a handy Templates section that features those used within the book, as well as ones that have proved to be popular with cardmakers.

A great many frustrations come about by not being able to find the items that you want. If you see the perfect embellishment on these pages and want to find a stockist, see our Resources Guide at the back. It will provide you with the contact details for the manufacturers as well as the UK or European distributors, who should be able to put you in contact with your nearest stockist.

The Complete Cardmaking Handbook

Getting started

There are some basics that are essential to every cardmaker's supplies stash – you are likely to use them over and over again, so it is worth investing in them at the start to make sure you are well equipped and raring to go.

Scissors One pair is a given, but really you should think about buying three or four different types. A large kitchen-type pair are fine for non-precision cutting. A small Teflon-coated pair are ideal for cutting anything sticky, and a very small precision-tip pair are perfect for all the fiddly jobs where you need to have pinpoint accuracy to achieve the neatest results.

Paper trimmer Also known as a guillotine, this is a must-have for straight lines. There are so many available, but a lightweight scrapbooker's trimmer is a good choice, as it has a 12" cutting area, and the cutting plate is levered so that you can slide lumpy embellishments underneath. It is flat, so perfect to store in a craft box.

Tweezers Such a simple tool, yet they will make your life so much easier. You do not need to buy craft ones, although they do have much longer arms so can be easier to use.

Bone folder The only way to guarantee clean, sharp folds.

Adhesives There's a mind-boggling array of glues on the market, half of which you will probably end up with in your stash. But to start with, you'll need double-sided sticky tape, which can be trimmed easily to size. 3D foam tape or pads add dimension, and a roller glue is easy to dispense and will not make your fingers sticky (a repositionable one is best, just in case you change your mind!). Dimensional glossy adhesive attaches stacks of different embellishments and dries clear.

Pencil A good old-fashioned HB pencil is a must for marking and drawing round templates. This goes hand in hand with a soft eraser.

Ruler A 30cm metal ruler is perfect for measuring, drawing and for use with a craft knife in straight-line cutting.

Cutting mat You'll need two different types of cutting surface: *Self-healing cutting mat* Suitable for cutting, piercing and setting eyelets.
Teflon-coated craft mat This is not just a baking sheet, as the craft ones are infused with glass that makes them stronger and also means that they will be able to be heated up to 650°C. The surface is 100% non-stick and is suitable for everything but cutting and setting.

Craft knife There are many different types of knife available, and they prove to be indispensable when it comes to cutting and scoring. Invest in one that has a changeable blade, as this will save you money in the long run.

All you need to do now is clear your work surface and begin the fun. Don't be disheartened if a technique doesn't work first time for you – often the best results are the unexpected ones.

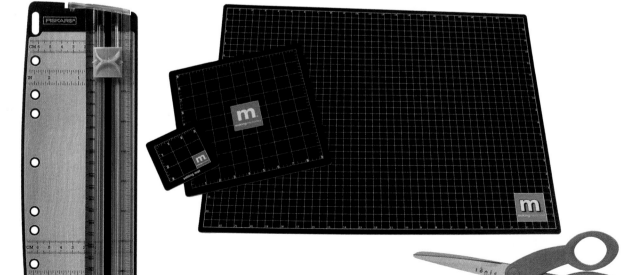

If you are unsure of anything, visit our online forum at www.practicalpublishing.co.uk where you'll find many talented and friendly cardmakers who are always happy to share their thoughts and ideas

Resist

Folding

Metal & Wire

Haberdashery

Altered

Celebrate

Seasonal

Theory

Before you start creating with all the wonderful techniques and products cardmaking has to offer, it's well worth getting to grips with the fundamentals behind any successful art project. These are **colour** and **design**.

This section will guide you through everything you need to know to create cards to a professional standard. With examples given throughout, it should be straightforward to understand the basic principles at work, and how they translate to your cardmaking.

There's a lot of information here, so don't feel disheartened if you don't get it all in one go. After an initial read-through, try putting certain elements into practice, as it's only when you see for yourself how it all works that you'll fully take it in.

But it's definitely worth the effort, and in the long run you'll save time and money by making sure that you get it right every time.

Colour

Warm or cold, clashing or co-ordinating – colours are integral to every craft project. Sometimes fortune favours the brave, but there are some general dos and don'ts that will help you come up trumps every time

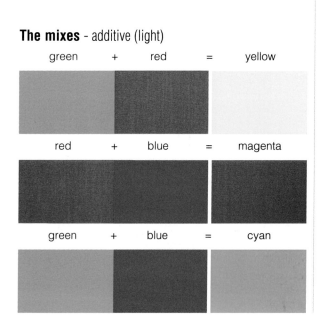

The theory of colour all started with Sir Isaac Newton, the first scientist to analyse light. He found that by passing a beam of light through a triangular prism, seven individually coloured rays of light emerged from the other side. Placing a second prism in the path of these seven rays had the effect of mixing the colours again, and what emerged from this second prism was once more a single beam of light.

We know that the three primary colours are red, yellow and blue. When mixed together, red and yellow make orange, red and blue make purple and yellow and blue make green. But there is another set of primary colours: red, blue and green. If you mix green and red light you get yellow; red and blue make magenta; green and blue make cyan.

Jargon busting

The red, yellow and blue primaries are those appertaining to pigment (paint), and the green, red and blue primaries are those appertaining to coloured light. The pigment primaries are called **subtractive** and the light primaries are called **additive**. Therefore, subtractive colour is obtained by mixing paints, and the additive colour by mixing together coloured light. If the three additive primaries are mixed together the ultimate effect is white (light), and a mixture of the three subtractive primaries produces black. For the rest of this article, when referring to primary colours we mean the subtractive primaries red, yellow and blue.

The definition of a true **primary** colour is one that cannot be mixed from any combination of any other two or more colours. It contains no trace of any other colour and appears visibly pure. A **secondary** colour is achieved by mixing together two primary colours. A **tertiary** colour is formed by mixing together a secondary colour with a primary one, or mixing together two secondary colours.

Another two words you may hear are **chromatic** and **achromatic**. The latter consists of black, white and greys. All other sources of colour, such as red, blue, green, yellow etc, are known as chromatic colours.

Other common words that you may be familiar with are hue, value and chroma. **Hue** is the quality that distinguishes one colour family from another: for example, red from blue, green from yellow and so on. **Value** is the

The mixes - subtractive (paint)

red	+	yellow	=	orange

red	+	blue	=	purple

yellow	+	blue	=	green

The mixes - additive (light)

green	+	red	=	yellow

red	+	blue	=	magenta

green	+	blue	=	cyan

Theory

quality that distinguishes between the lightness and darkness of a colour, such as light blue and dark blue. **Chroma** also refers to quality, but that which determines the strength or purity of a colour, such as a bright, pure yellow or a dull, greyed yellow.

Tints are chromatic colours to which a quantity of white has been added. If we take a pure colour such as red and add some white to it, however small this quantity may be, it will make the colour lighter in tone than the original, and it becomes a tint. Adding black to a pure colour forms a **shade**. Pink cannot be a shade of red because it is achieved by adding white to red, not black! **Pastel**

colours are achieved by adding equal quantities of black and white to a pure colour, making greyer, softer colours.

Hot and cold

Temperature and colour have a strong relationship, and it is common to refer to certain colours as being warm and to others as being cool. The colour circle in the natural order of colour can be simply divided into two distinct halves by drawing a line through from yellow to purple. Those hues to the left of this line – yellow, orange, red and purple – are known as **warm colours**, and those to the right – yellow, green, blue and lilac – are known as **cool colours**.

When light strikes a surface, it's either reflected or absorbed – and the rays that are absorbed are turned into energy or heat. This can be demonstrated by painting two identical pieces of metal, one white and one black, and placing them in direct sunlight. The white surface will reflect the light, absorbing none; the black will not only absorb all the light, but will also turn it into heat. If you were to touch the samples, you would find the black one significantly hotter than the white one.

A triadic colour scheme

Scheming

The six most common basic colour schemes – used in all sorts of industries, including cardmaking, scrapbooking and interior design – are monochromatic, complementary, analogous, split complementary, triadic and tetradic.

As the name suggests, a **monochromatic** colour scheme consists of different tints and shades of the same hue. Variety within the one colour of a monochromatic scheme can be achieved by the use of texture, form and pattern.

Whereas a monochromatic scheme is restricted to one basic hue, a **complementary** scheme uses two colours that are opposite each other on the colour wheel.

The most successful of **analogous** schemes are based upon two or three adjacent colours on the wheel. These tend to work nicely together because they are similar to each other in hue and contain

some of the same pure colours. And if you're feeling adventurous, an analogous scheme can successfully incorporate an accent of the colour complementary to the central hue of the analogous range while still remaining harmonious.

A **split complementary** scheme is based upon one hue, plus the two hues on either side of the first hue's complementary hue. This provides a less contrasting combination than complementary, while adding the variety of a further colour.

As its name suggests, a **triadic** scheme also involves three hues, but in this instance they are spaced equidistantly around the colour wheel.

As with triadic, the **tetradic** scheme speaks for itself. It's based on four hues that are equidistantly spaced on the colour wheel.

Defining colour

primary Cannot be mixed from any combination of any other two or more colours. Contains no visible trace of any other colour
secondary A mix of two primary colours
tertiary A mix of a secondary colour with a primary colour, or of two secondary colours

Theory

Elements of Design

You may not realise it, but chances are you're using these in your cardmaking already. Read on to make sure you're making the most of these central design themes...

There are seven elements of design that are used in all types of design work, from graphic and interior design, through cardmaking, to scrapbooking.

The seven elements are:

1. Point
2. Line
3. Form/Shape/Space
4. Movement
5. Colour
6. Pattern
7. Texture

We take each one in turn and break it down into digestible pieces, so why not grab a cuppa and put your feet up for a good read...

Point – here the eye is drawn to the embellishment

1. Point

Even if your card has just the one **point** (image, embellishment etc), there's something built into the brain that tries to find relationship or order, if only to use it as a point of orientation in relation to the outline of the page. If there are two points, the eye immediately makes a connection and 'sees' a line. If there are three points, then it is automatic to interpret them as a triangle, and so on. See how the eye is drawn towards the embellished corner of the pink Memories card.

One of the often-used rules in design is the **rule of thirds**. This can easily be applied to your cardmaking, as cards are generally square or rectangular.

Imaginary lines divide the project into thirds both horizontally and vertically. Important elements of your composition, such as embellishments, are placed where these lines intersect.

As well as using the intersections, you can arrange areas into bands occupying a third, or place things along the imaginary lines. Good locations to place decorations include a third of the way up, a third of the way in from the left – you get the idea. It doesn't work so well to put things centrally, at the top, at the bottom, or away in the corner. Using the rule of thirds helps produce nicely balanced projects. But once you've got the hang of it, you'll quickly want to break it! See how the Peace card and the Reflection, Enchantment, Harmony card use the central third for their main embellishment.

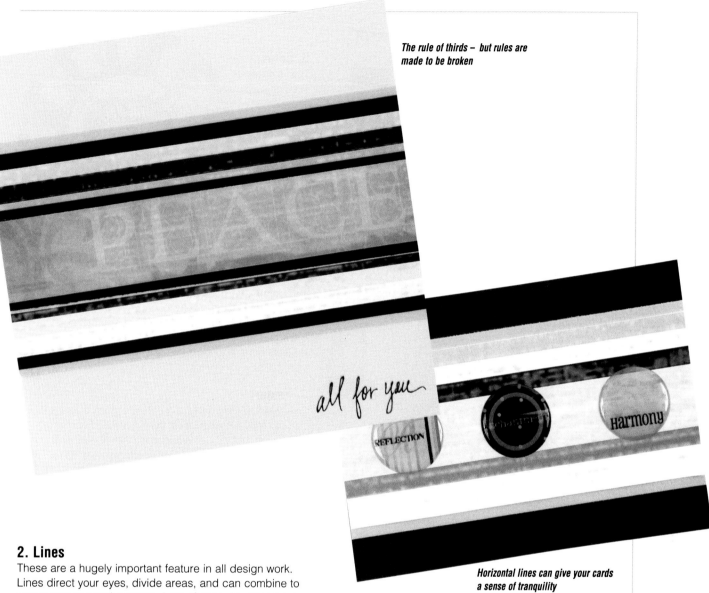

The rule of thirds – but rules are made to be broken

all for you

Horizontal lines can give your cards a sense of tranquility

2. Lines

These are a hugely important feature in all design work. Lines direct your eyes, divide areas, and can combine to create textures and patterns. Lots of everyday things are interpreted with lines, from underground tube station maps to the branches of a tree. Horizontal lines tend to intimate rest, quiet and relaxation, whilst vertical lines intimate greatness and stature. Diagonal ones suggest movement and direction, whilst curves can be soft and shallow or deep and acute, each evoking different moods. Again, the Peace and Reflection cards draw your eye across the centre, whilst the card with the silver heart uses the spotty ribbon to separate the two different papers.

3. Form/Shape/Space

These refer to a self-contained area of geometric or organic form that can either be two- or three-dimensional. **Geometric forms** are regular shapes, such as squares, circles, rectangles etc. There has definitely been a shift this year in papercrafts towards all things retro, which has associations with geometric shapes, especially circles. **Organic forms** tend to be irregular in outline.

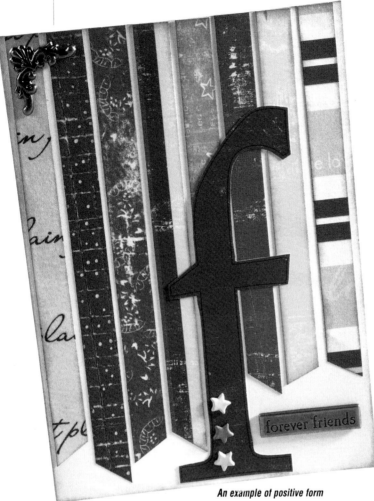

An example of positive form

5. Colour

This is covered in some detail in the preceding pages.

6. Pattern

Described as a repeating unit of shape or form, patterns can be found on a huge rainbow of papers out there today, from soft and subtle to bright and retro.

Using patterned papers on your cards adds interest and depth, and does most of the decoration for you. You can also make your own with a mixture of media such as inks, pens, chalks, stamps and paint. You can see that patterned papers have been used as accents for all the projects here, but you could use whole sheets to make your cards.

7. Texture

This refers to the quality of an object, which we sense through touch. It exists as a literal surface either that we can feel or that we can see and imagine the sensation we might feel. Smooth, soft, rough, hard, wet, dry – these are all common textures.

You can incorporate texture into your crafts by adding embellishments, fibres, ribbons, wood, textured paper, or anything that is tactile. There are lots of toppers and embellishments available to buy that address this element for you, and most paper manufacturers have brought out new textured card lines. Craftwork Cards has also released a new set of textured blank pre-scored cards, together with A4 packs, in a multitude of beautiful colours to match its range. All the card used in these projects is textured, but more texture has been added by way of embellishments, such as epoxy stickers, wax seals, flowers and ribbon.

You can also have **abstract form**, which would include caricatures or cartoon images, which are often used in stamping art.

Form can be **positive** or **negative**. Negative form is often used with lettering, where, after you cut out a letter and use it in a greeting, instead of throwing away the piece of paper that the letter has been cut from, you incorporate this into your cards too. This is popular in papercrafting at the moment, with the use of monograms and stencils.

4. Movement

Kinetics (the science of forces to create motion) is another element of papercraft that is becoming increasingly popular.

Moving pieces on cards can include tags, envelopes, dials and pop-up images. Hiding messages under a flap or making the recipient untie a bow to open the card are all ways of incorporating movement and adding an enticing interactive element.

Your cardmaking can also take on a three-dimensional form, for example by using decoupage, wire creations or overlapping items.
Space creates depth and dimension while adding interest, excitement and contrast. Don't clutter your work with too many different elements, though, as this will lead to a confused look. Try to remember to put warm colours in front of dark ones, as cool colours naturally recede.

Principles of Design

Whereas the elements are the very components of design, the principles affect the arrangement of these components on your cards. Representing the roots of design practice, they will help you to make top-notch cards every time

There are five principles of design, which we will again take in turn:

1. **Balance**
2. **Proportion**
3. **Rhythm**
4. **Emphasis/dominance**
5. **Unity**

1. Balance

The concept of visual equilibrium relates to our physical sense of balance. Most successful compositions achieve balance in one of two ways: symmetrically or asymmetrically. Balance in a three-dimensional object is easy to understand, as if balance isn't achieved, the object tips over. But how is this determined two-dimensionally?

Symmetrical balance, also known as **formal balance**, occurs when the weight of a composition is evenly distributed around a central vertical or horizontal axis. Under normal circumstances it assumes identical forms on both sides of the axis. The It's A Girl card has a horizontal symmetry in so far as if you were to look at the patterned paper, it's the same above the horizon as it is below. If you look at the Girl Flower card on the following page, the patterned paper again has vertical symmetry. It is also possible to have a composition that is symmetrical around a central point, which is known as **radial symmetry**.

Asymmetrical balance, also known as **informal balance**, occurs when the weight of a composition isn't evenly distributed around a central axis. It involves the

Symmetrical balance   *Asymmetrical balance*

Theory

arrangement of objects of differing size in a composition, such that they balance one another with their respective visual weights. Often there is one dominant form offset by many smaller forms. A good example of asymmetrical balance is the Baby Girl card on the previous page. You can see that the large spotted circle is the most dominant element, but this is balanced above the horizon by two metal plaques and a knot in the ribbon.

2. Proportion

This refers to the relative size and scale of the various elements in a design. It is the relationship in scale between one element and another, or between a whole object and one of its parts. You'll find that large pieces of your project come to the front, whilst smaller articles or embellishments seem to recede into the background.

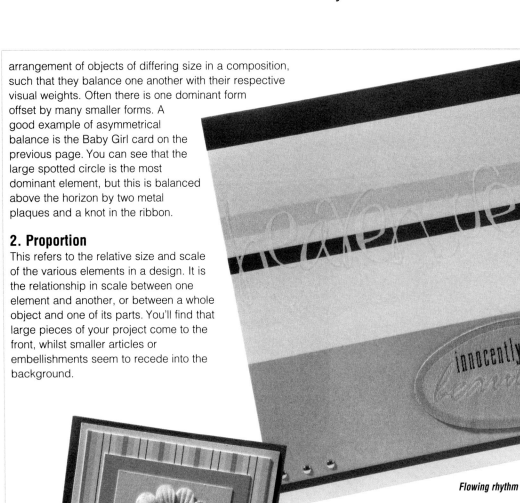

Flowing rhythm

Regular rhythm

3. Rhythm

Rhythm is the repetition or alternation of elements, often with defined intervals between them. It creates a sense of movement, and can establish pattern and texture. There are many different kinds of rhythm, often defined by the feeling evoked when looking at the elements.

Regular rhythm occurs when the intervals between the elements, and often the elements themselves, are similar in size or length. Look at the Girl Flower card, where you have three squares all of the same size with the same distance between them.

Flowing rhythm gives a sense of movement. You can see that on the Heaven Sent card and the Little One card: on both the cards, you look first at the rub-on wording then down to the label or the flower – the embellishments move your gaze.

4. Emphasis/Dominance

A **point of focus** marks the location in a composition that most strongly draws the viewer's attention. There's usually a main or **primary point of emphasis** with sometimes **secondary** and **tertiary emphases** in other parts of the composition. The emphasis is usually an

The Complete Cardmaking Handbook

*The primary point of emphasis
here is the photograph of the baby*

*Primary, secondary and
tertiary emphases*

interruption in the fundamental pattern or movement of the viewer's eye through the composition, or a break in the rhythm. In terms of cardmaking, you would use emphasis to call attention to a stamped image or a greeting, for example. On the Little One card, the most dominant element is the title, whilst the secondary emphasis is the flower, and the tertiary, the background paper.

Emphasis can be achieved in a number of ways. Repetition creates it by calling attention to the repeated element through sheer force of numbers, as in the Girl Flower card. A contrast of colour, texture or shape will also call attention to a specific point, as will contrast of size or scale. Placement in a strategic position will stress a particular element of a design.

5. Unity

The underlying principle that summarises all of the principles and elements of design, unity is concerned with the aspects of a given design that are necessary to tie the composition together, to give it a sense of wholeness, or to break it apart and give it variety.

Onwards and upwards!

Armed with all your new information on colour theory and the elements and principles of design, you'll begin to understand why sometimes you get things spot on, and sometimes they just look wrong. If your creativity is hitting a wall and you can't work out why a card won't come together, refer back to this article and you're sure to be able to explain it away

Tools for the job

✿ stickers
✿ craft knife
✿ tweezers
✿ 3D foam pads
✿ scissors
✿ cardstock

Stickers

Traditionally thought of as an embellishment favoured by children, stickers are the ultimate quick fix. But our designers show that they deserve more attention than you might at first give them

Stickers are possibly the most readily available embellishment that can be used in cardmaking. Coming in almost every conceivable design, colour and shape, they can be purchased with different-coloured backgrounds and also in a transparent vellum style. The quality and the adhesives vary from brand to brand. A sticker can be used to form an entire card, or as an accent. They are also a handy way of adding dimension, be it a greeting or sentiment, or an image. Although these adhesive treats can be a quick and simple approach to a card, they can equally form part of a more intricate design.

Thinking of You
by Mrs M Ward

Materials:

☐ Adirondack purple inkpad
☐ white card blank
☐ Do Crafts stickers
☐ purple gingham paper
☐ yellow & purple pearlescent paper
☐ organza ribbon
☐ Anita's stamp

To create:

1 Select stickers and mount onto squares of colour co-ordinated card.

2 Position and attach the squares onto the patterned paper, using 3D foam for the central design.

3 Matt the gingham paper onto pearlescent paper, leaving a border. Tie the ribbon around this and add a bow, adhering it on the reverse.

4 Attach the matted design to the card blank and stamp the message using the purple ink.

step 1 *Carefully peel your chosen design from the backing sheet, taking care at the edges. You could use tweezers if it's particularly small and fiddly.*

step 2 *Stick onto your cardstock or paper, then cut around the design using your craft knife or scissors.*

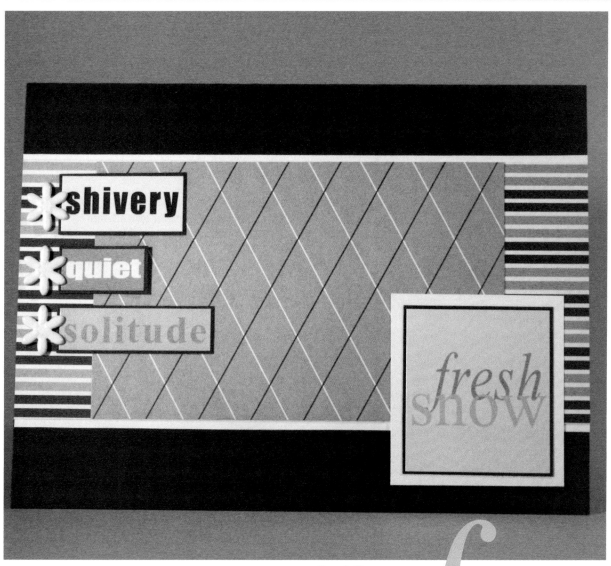

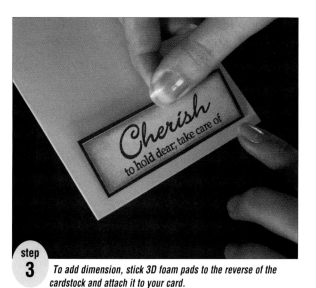

step 3 To add dimension, stick 3D foam pads to the reverse of the cardstock and attach it to your card.

Fresh Snow
by Christi Snow

Materials:
☐ Pebbles Inc. Straight Talk Sampler Winter sticker
☐ Tree House Memories Zach Criss Cross Diamond patterned paper
☐ Tree House Memories Zach Lollipop Sticks patterned paper
☐ white & navy blue cardstock
☐ brads

To create:
1. Trim the patterned papers to fit into the central section of the card.
2. Mount onto white card leaving a narrow border showing on the top and the bottom.
3. Mount all the stickers onto navy blue card, then mount the main sticker onto an additional layer of white card.
4. Attach the stickers with the white brads.

(i) A sticker is a piece of paper with a sticky side, hence its name. This side is usually made of a gluey substance that adheres to objects and surfaces. In the craft industry, stickers are decorated with printed images and fonts

Tools for the job
- ✿ peel-offs
- ✿ craft knife
- ✿ tweezers
- ✿ low-tack tape

Stick & Quick

Peel-offs

One of the best-selling cardmaking items, most shops struggle to keep well stocked with this cardmaker's essential

Peel-offs are easy to use, but some crafters have a phobia towards them, believing they make projects look last minute. But these little gems are so versatile it would be wrong to dismiss them. Traditionally made in gold or silver, and used to express a greeting as a finishing touch, they have developed dramatically over the last few years, and are now available in almost any shape, colour and design.

Peel-offs can be used as simple stickers, though they are also perfect for creating dimensional shapes, for use as templates, and for masking (see page 86). As well as this, peel-offs can be coloured or painted. They are delicate and intricate, and need to be handled carefully or they can tear or become misshapen. This can be resolved by handling the peel-off with tweezers and placing low-tack tape across the sticker before you remove it from the backing sheet. This will allow you to position the peel-off without it losing its shape, so no more wonky words!

Happy Birthday
by Jill Atrill

Materials:
- ☐ Prism lilac card
- ☐ purple pearlescent paper
- ☐ purple handmade paper
- ☐ translucent butterfly
- ☐ vellum
- ☐ silver border, Happy Birthday & Best Wishes peel-offs
- ☐ silver Japanese-themed peel-offs
- ☐ small purple flower brad

To create:

1 Cut out the screen using the template, then cut windows from the two central pieces with a craft knife. Keep the offcuts. Score and fold the screen.

2 Print images onto the vellum and fit these behind the two windows.

3 Use the cutouts from the windows to trace two arches onto the pearlescent paper. Stick these to the outside panels.

4 Make an origami kimono out of handmade paper. Create 3D shapes using peel-offs and foam pads. Attach all the elements, edge with the peel-off borders and finish off with greetings.

step 1 *Place a low-tack tape over the peel-off that you've selected.*

step 2 *Peel off the backing tape using a craft knife and a pair of tweezers. Take care at the corners or any intricate parts.*

Birthday Wishes Castle
by Dawn Taylor

Materials:
- ☐ pink & white glitter cardstock
- ☐ Anita's Sticky Ribbons
- ☐ silver border peel-offs
- ☐ Funky Foam in a variety of colours
- ☐ white cardstock
- ☐ cocktail sticks
- ☐ bead

To create:

1. Draw a template of the desired castle. This example is A5 size with: back page with one tower and two turrets; middle page with four turrets; front page with two towers and one gate. Draw around the template onto glittered card and cut it out.

2. Cut out: triangles of pink and purple funky foam for the turrets; long scalloped rectangles and smaller rectangles for the top of the towers; tiny rectangles for bricks; and a border wide enough to fit between the two front towers to make the frame of the gate.

3. Arrange all the shapes on the card. Make a slit in the front card between the towers to form a gate. Place a piece of white card with silver mesh on it behind the opening, so that it gives a grate effect.

4. Cut out window shapes from white funky foam and place silver peel-offs on the foam to create windows. Cut grass out of green foam and attach this to the bottom of the first card. Fix silver ribbon to the turrets.

5. Glue a pink bead to the end of a small cocktail stick, attach a greeting in the shape of a flag, and secure the stick to the back of the card.

6. Fold four 2x6cm rectangles of paper into quarters and unfold them. Use these to make two concertinas and stick one at either side, between the front and middle sheets of card, in order to to create a space between each sheet when the card is standing.

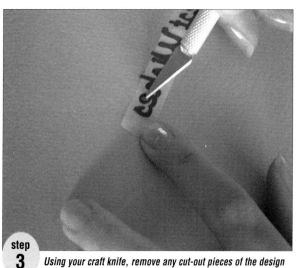

step 3 *Using your craft knife, remove any cut-out pieces of the design that didn't stay on the backing sheet.*

step 4 *Position the shape or word where you want it to appear. Take care not to stick it in the wrong place. Once positioned, peel off the low-tack tape.*

ⓘ **Peel-offs are embossed outline stickers created in metallic paper. They are traditionally a word or greeting**

Happy Birthday
by Heather Bryant

Materials:
- ☐ textured cream cardstock
- ☐ Hot Off The Press gingham paper
- ☐ gold mirri card
- ☐ gold vases, butterflies & greetings outline peel-offs
- ☐ Anita's Sticky Ribbons
- ☐ Pebbles Inc. chalks
- ☐ Colour Play 3D paints
- ☐ yellow glitter card
- ☐ yellow material butterflies
- ☐ cream cardstock

To create:

1. Score and fold the cream cardstock to create your card. Trim 2cm from one edge using decorative scissors; stick the cut-off piece inside the card on the outside edge.

2. Stick the vase outline sticker to the cream cardstock, colour the flowers and leaves with 3D paint, then shade the vases with chalks. Matt onto the mirri card then onto patterned paper, trimming with decorative scissors.

3. Follow the above step for the Happy Birthday block. Adhere both pieces to the card. Attach the ribbon down the side of the card.

4. Stick and matt the embellishments as shown. To create the 3D butterflies, stick three peel-off butterflies wing-to-wing and, using the open sides, stick them to the card.

Musical Tag
by Natalie O'Shea

Materials:
- ☐ pearlescent bronze & gold card
- ☐ Prism black & cream cardstock
- ☐ black musical instruments peel-offs
- ☐ acetate
- ☐ gold leaf pen
- ☐ gold leaf sheet
- ☐ gold raffia ribbon

To create:

1 Stick peel-off drums onto acetate. Apply size to the back of the acetate, then apply the gold leaf. When dry, trim around the edges of the drums.

2 Cut the cream card into a tag shape, and attach the drums and additional peel-offs. Edge with the gold leafing pen. Thread the gold raffia through the hole.

3 Mount onto black card and edge with deckle-edged scissors.

4 Cut a square of gold pearlescent cardstock to the base card, attach the tag at an angle and finish with a few additional outline stickers.

40
by Stephanie Maynard

Materials:
- ☐ cream card blank
- ☐ Prism green cardstock
- ☐ holographic green paper
- ☐ holographic letters & stars peel-offs
- ☐ silver peel-off borders
- ☐ green bow
- ☐ wire

To create:

1 Cut a rectangle from the green card smaller than the front of the card. Adhere it to the card.

2 Cut a square and a small rectangle from the green holographic paper. Stick a cross of the border stickers onto the large square, and onto the small rectangle affix the number 40.

3 Attach the small rectangle to a piece of wire using tape. Sandwich one end of a piece of wire between two star peel-offs. Repeat this.

4 Fix the three wired embellishments behind the square with tape and attach the square to the card. Finish with additional stars on the background and a bow on the gift.

Tools for the job

✿ rub-ons
✿ wooden lolly stick
✿ scissors

Rub-ons

A relatively new addition to the papercrafter's kit are dry transfers. Used in the printing industry for mock-ups, they are a perfect addition to your cards

In 1960 a company called Letraset announced its revolutionary new product: instant lettering dry transfer. A revolution in graphic design, suddenly lettering could be done quickly and easily by anyone. The demand was enormous. Since then, the product has been developed and is now available in almost every colour (as well as metallic), and a huge range of fonts, sentiments, greetings and images.

Papercraft rub-ons are a quick and clean way of adding fonts and imagery to your designs, and they can be transferred onto a variety of mediums. The transparent backing sheet means that you can reposition the decal before attaching it to your card. Once you're happy with its position, the image can be transferred using a wooden lolly stick. Some will require more rubbing than others.

ℹ️ **Dry transfer is a term used to describe decals that can be applied without the use of water or other solvent. Sometimes they are called rub-ons or rubdowns due to the method of application. The decal itself is on a backing material such as paper or plastic sheeting. The backing is placed decal side down, on the surface to transfer to, then applied by rubbing with a stylus, wooden lollypop stick, ballpoint pen, pencil or similar object**

step 1 Cut your chosen letter, shape or word from the backing sheet. Position this in the location that you want the rub-on to appear. Place it gently in position, as the back of the rub-on is slightly sticky. You can reposition at this point until you are happy.

step 2 Press the rub-on onto the surface firmly, then rub the backing with a lolly stick or similar. As you rub, you should be able to see the backing lifting off the rub-on.

Cherish

by Louise Gilmour

Materials:

☐ cardstock
☐ Shabby Princess downloaded paper
☐ Making Memories metal words & safety pins
☐ Making Memories rub-ons
☐ Ornate stick-on jewels
☐ Brilliance inkpads (to colour brads)
☐ Making Memories brads & eyelets
☐ artificial flower heads
☐ sequin strip
☐ bracelet charm
☐ ribbons

To create:

1 Attach the patterned paper to the card, leaving a gap at one end. Adhere a strip of sequins along the edge.

2 Using the inkpad, colour the three brads then use these to attach the flowers to the card. Set four eyelets around the side and top of the card. Through these, thread and knot short pieces of ribbon.

3 Thread the charm onto the safety pin and fix that to the top ribbons. Use foam pads to adhere the metal word to the bottom of the card.

4 Finish off with the Cherish, Beginning and Welcome rub-ons and a few adhesive jewels.

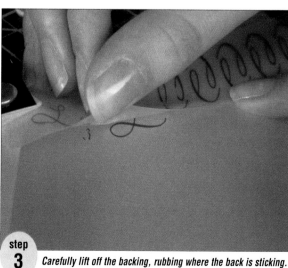

step 3 *Carefully lift off the backing, rubbing where the back is sticking.*

Thank You
by Lousette Ashton

Materials:
☐ A5 card
☐ Gin-X She Wears Pink patterned paper
☐ MAMBI So Girly hearts & flowers rub-ons
☐ K&Co Beyond Postmarks rub-ons
☐ dressmaker's tracing wheel

To create:
1 Fold an A5 card lengthways and cut 3.5cm from one end. Cover the top two thirds of the card with pink patterned paper and run a dressmaker's tracing wheel along the edges.

2 Cut three small rectangles from plasma and transfer a rub-on heart onto each one. Glue the rectangles into place with 3D pads, making sure the pads are hidden behind the images.

3 Finish off with a small message rub-on.

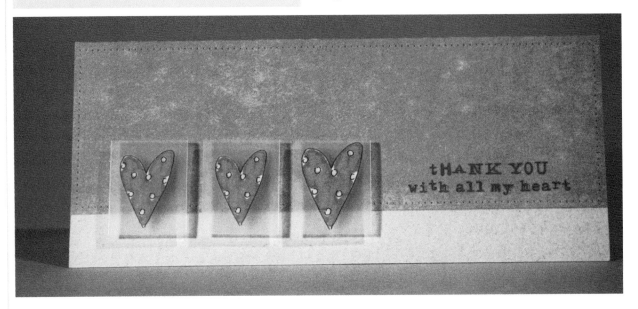

Eiffel Tower
by Christi Snow

Materials:
☐ Anna Griffin Roses patterned paper
☐ DCWV The Fall Stack cardstock
☐ Create-A-Collage Paris Collage rub-ons
☐ Pebbles Inc. brown chalk

To create:
1 Colour-block the base of the card and chalk the edges of each section with brown chalk.

2 Attach a small dark brown border between the sections. Apply the various Paris-themed rub-ons to the solid cardstock sections.

3 Finish the card with a small dark brown border added to the spine.

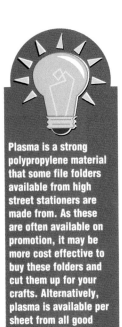

Plasma is a strong polypropylene material that some file folders available from high street stationers are made from. As these are often available on promotion, it may be more cost effective to buy these folders and cut them up for your crafts. Alternatively, plasma is available per sheet from all good craft suppliers

Always
by Penny Hajiantoni

Materials:
☐ Stampington stamp
☐ Making Memories suede frame
☐ BasicGrey patterned paper
☐ Adirondack Red Pepper & Oregano inkpads
☐ Dies To Die For blossoms
☐ Doodlebug stitches rub-ons
☐ button
☐ epoxy sticker
☐ greeny gold & cream cardstock
☐ card blank
☐ watercolours

To create:

1 Cut two pieces of patterned cardstock and two pieces of plain cardstock so that they create a patchwork on the card blank.

2 Using watercolours, stamp the image onto cream cardstock. Trim it to size and adhere it to the card. Fix the suede frame over it.

3 Attach the blossoms to the card and glue a button in the centre of the flower. Apply the epoxy sticker to the frame.

4 Cut lengths of the stitches rub-ons and apply in place between the patchwork pieces, as shown.

Tools for the job

✿ punch
✿ papers
✿ scissors
✿ pens or markers
✿ chalks

Punches

Punched shapes, or 'punchies' as they are more affectionately known, are a fun and easy way to add dimension to your cards and other papercrafts

Sweetie by Teresa Collins

unches are quick and easy to use, and produce a consistent shape to use in your designs. Punched shapes can be used in their raw form, or you can utilise the negative from your punch, which is a hot trend in crafts such as scrapbooking. Various punched shapes can be combined to create a dimensional accent for your card. Using paper punches, scissor tips and a little imagination, anyone can turn simple punched shapes into stunning works of art. Chalks and markers can be used to add to and embellish your punchies.

Invest in a punch and you will use it time and time again in your projects. Taking care of your punches will secure your investment and increase their longevity. If your punch is sticking, take a piece of wax/greaseproof paper and cut out shapes. Punching through this will lubricate the mechanisms. To keep your punch sharp and prevent furred edges on your cutouts, punching tinfoil or a low-grade sandpaper will sharpen the edges of both the male punch and female die. This will help you have quality cutouts for years to come.

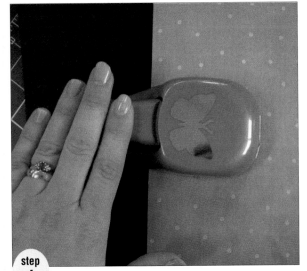

step 1 *Select your card or paper and punch your shapes. It can be easier to punch upside down as you can see where the shape will be cut.*

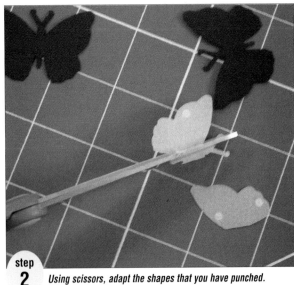

step 2 *Using scissors, adapt the shapes that you have punched.*

The Complete Cardmaking Handbook

Punch Art

Autumn
by Christi Snow

Materials:
- [ ] EK Success Whale of a Punch Leaf punch
- [ ] DCWV patterned paper & cardstock
- [ ] Junkitz Fall Expressionz rub-ons
- [ ] ribbon

To create:
1. Layer the base of the card. Punch the leaf in four different colours of cardstock and mount along the left edge of the card.
2. Punch a mini leaf and mount onto the lower-right corner of the card.
3. Trim a semicircle and rub on the title.
4. Attach the ribbons.

step 3
Shade your die-cut shapes using a palette of chalks, which will add depth and dimension.

step 4
Glue the shapes together, building them up to create 3D forms. Add finer details with pens.

> **i** A punch is a manually operated press used for forming holes or shapes. It consists of a male punch and a female die, which, when pressed together, will form a hole in a piece of paper that is of the same geometry as the punch

Happy Birthday
by Mavis Marsden

Materials:
- ☐ Prism white & pink cardstocks
- ☐ chalks
- ☐ Stickles silver & green glitter glues
- ☐ daisy punches
- ☐ butterfly die-cuts

To create:
Print the title onto the white card. Cut to size and chalk the edges.
Matt onto the gingham paper and adorn with punched shapes.
Decorate with glitter glue.

Hello
by Kirsty Wiseman

Materials:
- ☐ white textured cardstock
- ☐ Prism green & yellow cardstocks
- ☐ vellum
- ☐ letter & daisy stickers
- ☐ daisy punch
- ☐ green gems
- ☐ yellow eyelets
- ☐ embroidery floss
- ☐ buttons & ribbon

To create:
Score and fold the card and attach a yellow and green square onto the base, tearing at one end. Cut a tag from the green cardstock, and a square from vellum, and attach with eyelets.
Decorate the tag with letter stickers, thread and punched flowers. Tie a ribbon on the tag and attach the gems.
Finish and embellish with buttons and stickers.

Punch Art

Mum
by Kirsty Wiseman

To create:

1. Score and fold the cardstock to create a card blank. Punch three circles in the front of the card to create apertures.
2. Tear a strip of brown card, attach it to the left-hand side of the card, and tie the mesh ribbon around.
3. Decorate the circles with a variety of punched daisies. Adhere the letter stickers in the circles.

Materials:
☐ mottled cream cardstock
☐ circle punch
☐ small daisy punch
☐ Type Writer letter stickers
☐ mesh ribbon
☐ Prism brown cardstocks

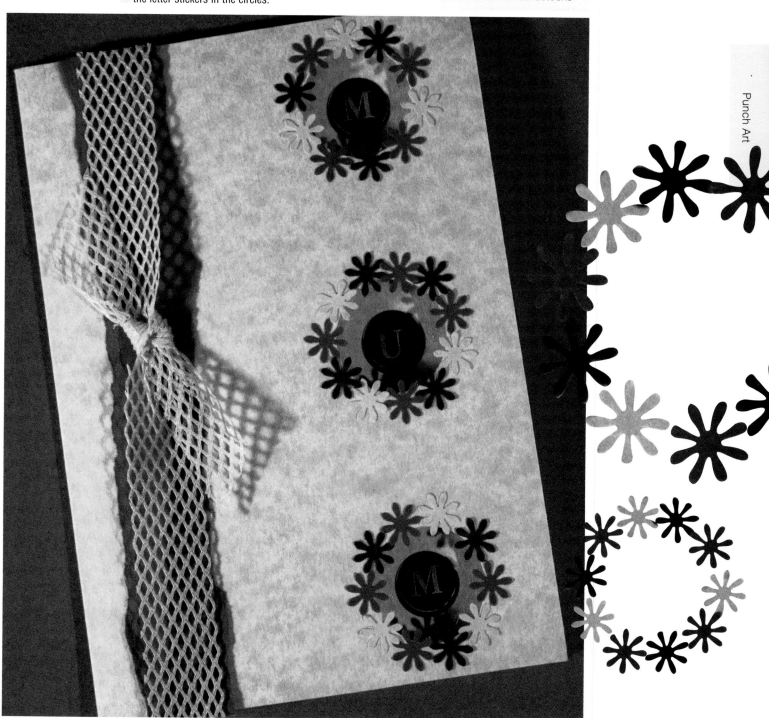

Tools for the job

✿ QuicKutz tool
✿ dies
✿ paper
✿ adhesives
✿ chalks (for shading)

Die-cuts

There are many different die-cutting systems on the market, so you're spoilt for choice when it comes to creating great little shapes

Die-cutting machines come in many different shapes and sizes. The smallest and most portable of them has to be the QuickKutz: a handheld tool that uses dies smaller than a credit card. Storage of die-cutters can be a big issue, but the QuickKutz (QK) fits away into a neat little folder. It works as many others do: a shaped metal die is pressed against paper by applying pressure to a die-cutting machine lever. This action creates a cutout. The dies are not sharp to the touch and are safe for children to use.

Die templates are available in almost every shape you could imagine, along with a variety of different fonts and textures. These can either be used in the straightforward shape that the die creates, or you can mix and merge these pieces to create fun and interesting designs.

Hope by Teresa Collins

step 1 *Select your die and insert it into the top of the jaws of the QK. It will stick to the magnetic plates.*

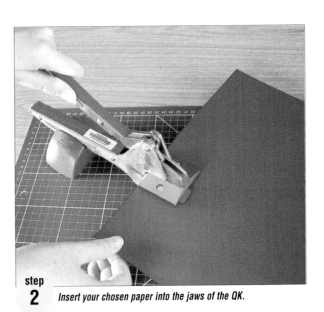

step 2 *Insert your chosen paper into the jaws of the QK.*

The Complete Cardmaking Handbook

Punch Art

Fill Your Life
by Katie Shanahan-Jones

Materials:
- ☐ QuicKutz Small, Medium & Large Daisy dies
- ☐ QuicKutz Ivy Leaves die
- ☐ QuicKutz Flower doodads die
- ☐ cream and deep red cardstock
- ☐ different shades of green cardstock

To create:
1. Print your phrase onto green cardstock using your computer and tear around the edges. Stick onto deep green card.

2. Cut two or three large QuicKutz daisies from cream and red cardstock. Also cut a selection of smaller flowers from cream and red, and cut ivy leaves from various shades of green.

3. Stick the leaves around the printed card, forming a frame on three sides. Alternate the sizes and shades.

4. Next, stick two or three of the large daisies on the card, swapping the centres between the colours. Now stick the rest of the daisies in place, filling in the gaps as you go.

Fill your Life with Sunshine and your Heart with Love.

step 3 *Remove the paper and pop out the die-cut shape.*

> **ⓘ** **Die-cutting is the process of using specially designed cutting tools to create custom shapes or cutouts in paper, cardstock or any other material you manage to punch through!**

Merry Mitmas
by Kirsty Wiseman

Materials:
☐ patterned paper
☐ white card blank
☐ Prism red, blue & green cardstocks
☐ 3D foam tabs
☐ ribbon
☐ hat, scarf & mittens die

To create:
Die-cut the shapes using different colours of cardstock.

From patterned paper, cut out three squares and attach these centrally to the card blank.

Attach the die-cut shapes onto the squares using 3D foam pads. Punch three holes in the top-right corner of the card and tie ribbon through.

Finish off with a printed title matted on the patterned paper.

If your dies start to cut with a furry edge, cut into fine-grade sandpaper, which sharpens the edges of your die

Punch Art

Happy Birthday
by Lousette Ashton

Materials:
- ☐ white card blank
- ☐ Prism cardstock in white & various shades of blue
- ☐ patterned paper
- ☐ ribbon
- ☐ Making Memories rub-ons
- ☐ flower, bookplate & font dies

To create:

Cut the flowers, bookplate and birthday letters from the various cardstocks.

Tear a piece of patterned paper to the size of the card blank and adhere the bookplate to this with 3D foam pads. Using this as a template, cut the card behind the bookplate to create an aperture.

Adhere the ribbon and letters to the outside of the card, and embellish the inside with cardstock and the flowers, so that the design shows through the aperture.

Finish off with the rub-ons.

Have Fun
by Louise Gilmour

Materials:
- ☐ Prism cardstock in blue, black, pink, green & white
- ☐ QuicKutz Ladybug & metal-rimmed tag dies
- ☐ Making Memories rub-ons
- ☐ black craft wire
- ☐ diamanté gems

To create:

Punch using your QK ladybugs and a variety of circles. Score and fold blue cardstock to make your card blank.

Assemble the ladybugs (cutting off the antennae) and adhere the circle in a varied pattern on the white cardstock. Trim a strip for the front of the card.

Create two strips of cardstock: one in pink and one in green. Adhere these to the back of the circle-patterned cardstock. Trim the edges using a tracing wheel.

Create antennae from black craft wire then assemble the card as shown, adhering the gems and rub-ons to finish.

Punch Art

Spotty Puppy
by Katie Shanahan-Jones

Materials:
- ☐ cream cardstock
- ☐ Sandy Lion Blue's Clues stickers
- ☐ QuicKutz Grass die
- ☐ QuicKutz Flower doodads die

To create:

Take a 12x6" piece of cream cardstock. Use a bone folder to score across the width of the card at 4" intervals, then fold along the score lines. Your card will now fold into three sections of 4", like a concertina.

Use character stickers like these Blue's Clues ones. First, fold the card up so you know which side of the panels to apply the stickers to. Stick the largest sticker (Blue) to the back panel of the card. Apply another character (the green puppy) to the middle panel, then Periwinkle on the front panel. When the card is unfolded and standing up, you'll be able to see all three characters at once.

There are plenty of small stickers, flowers, butterflies etc on the sticker sheet – add these around your characters. Across the bottom of the card, affix some grass die-cuts in shades of green and some extra flower die-cuts.

Cut the cardstock carefully around the upper sections of the stickers, making sure to leave a narrow border of cardstock showing.

Pink & Flowery
by Katie Shanahan-Jones

Materials:
- ☐ pink 4x6" card
- ☐ Chatterbox paper
- ☐ BasicGrey paper
- ☐ QuicKutz Small, Medium & Large Daisy dies

To create:

Take two pieces of toning pink patterned paper, one light (Chatterbox) and one dark pink (BasicGrey). Trim them both so they measure 3.5x5.5".

Stick the dark pink piece of patterned paper centrally onto the pink 4x6" card.

Line the light pink patterned paper over the dark pink piece without sticking it. Tear the light pink paper diagonally from the top-right to the bottom-left corner. Stick this triangular piece of paper onto the left-hand side of the card.

Cut three large daisy die-cuts and four small daisy die-cuts in shades of pink and cream. Swap the middles of the flowers around.

Stick the daisies onto the card – odd numbers work best.

Girls Get Together Invite
by Katie Shanahan-Jones

Materials:
- ☐ purple cardstock
- ☐ Chatterbox papers
- ☐ QuicKutz Handbag die
- ☐ 4 seed beads
- ☐ Sparkly font free from Fontdiner.com

To create:
Print out your invitation in the Sparkly font. Cut a piece of purple cardstock that measures 1" wider and stick the invite to it.

Using the QuicKutz handbag, die-cut four shapes from four different Chatterbox papers. Put the die-cuts through your mini Xyron to apply adhesive.

Stick the handbags on the four corners of the invite then stick the handbag flaps onto each bag.

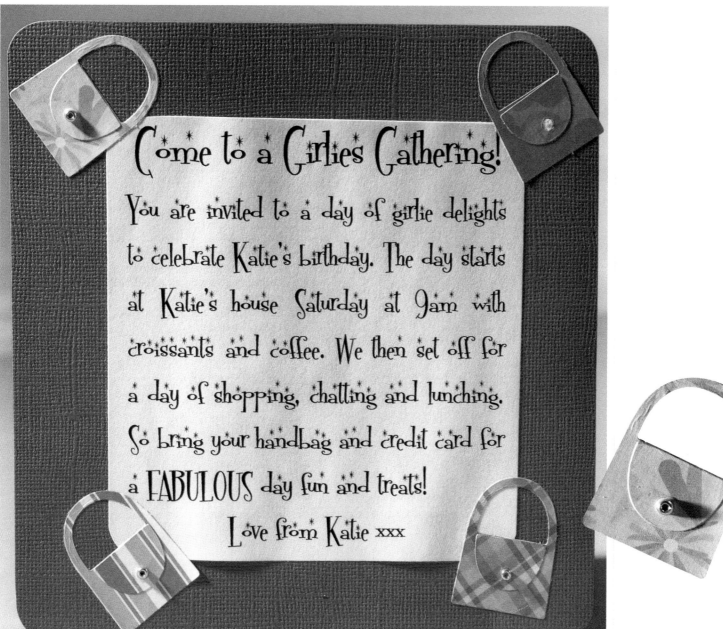

Come to a Girlies Gathering!

You are invited to a day of girlie delights to celebrate Katie's birthday. The day starts at Katie's house Saturday at 9am with croissants and coffee. We then set off for a day of shopping, chatting and lunching. So bring your handbag and credit card for a FABULOUS day fun and treats!

Love from Katie xxx

Tools for the job

❀ lightbox or sunny window

❀ stylus

❀ tape
❀ brass template
❀ paper or cardstock
❀ waxed paper

Embossing

Dry-embossing

Creating texture or a relief in paper gives an elegant and beautiful finish to almost any greetings card. It is a simple technique, and while the templates can be expensive, it is possible to create you own

Embossing is the process of carving a relief, or texture, into a material. In this instance, it is known as dry-embossing, and the carving is made into paper or cardstock. Dry, or relief, embossing is done by tracing a stencil with a special tool, called a stylus, which looks like a metal pen with a rounded metal ball at the nib. Using the stylus, you trace the outline of the pattern, taking care not to press too hard and rip the paper. The result is a stunning pattern that jumps out from the page.

Dry-embossing can be done an almost all paper mediums. However, it is recommended that on some papers you rub over a wax paper, which assists the stylus to move more smoothly over the project. You can emboss on all kinds of surfaces, including metal! The variety of templates is amazing, and you can use brass, plastic or homemade ones.

Christmas
by Natalie O'Shea

Materials:
☐ silver card
☐ pale blue card
☐ eyelet
☐ organza ribbon
☐ peel-off greeting
☐ double-sided tape
☐ glitter
☐ Kars striped stencil
☐ Christmas tree stencil
☐ tag stencil

To create:

1 Use some silver card and emboss the stripes. Attach diagonally to the front of your card and trim to size.

2 Emboss a tag, trim, and add some organza ribbon with an eyelet. Attach a peel-off greeting to some blue card, trim and attach to the centre of the tag. Secure the tag at an angle over the striped pattern.

3 Attach some double-sided tape along the striped edge and shake glitter over the tap, shaking off the excess.

4 Emboss a Christmas tree, trim, and attach using 3D foam pads to the top-right corner of your card.

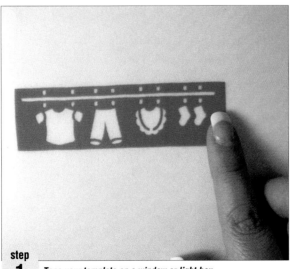

step 1 *Tape your template on a window or light box. Stencils are avaiable in metal or plastic*

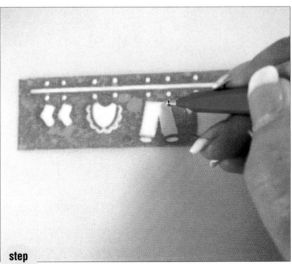

step 2 *Using the stylus to gently press the paper into the template. Use the large tip and work your way around the outline of the design.*

Embossing

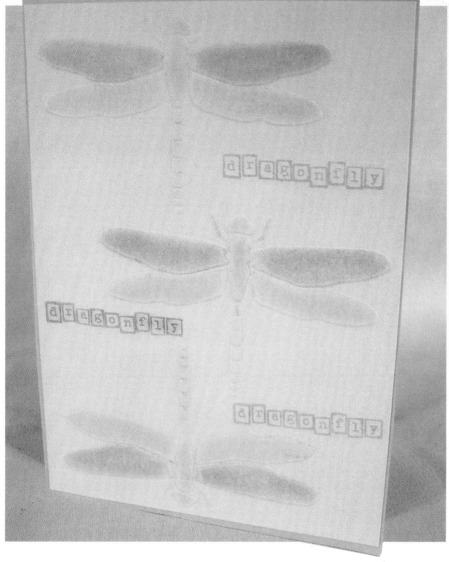

Dragonfly
by Sue Roddis

Materials:
☐ A5 purple cardstock
☐ cream cardstock
☐ masking tape
☐ Dream Weaver Dragonfly stencil LM193
☐ I kan'dee chalks
☐ Stampers Anonymous Dragonfly stamp
☐ VersaMark

To create:

1 Using a lightbox and embossing template, emboss three dragonflies on the cream card. Score and fold the A5 cardstock, and cut the cream cardstock to fit.

2 Colour the dragonflies with the chalks. Stamp the dragonfly title stamp three times using the VersaMark inkpad and colour with chalks.

3 Assemble the card.

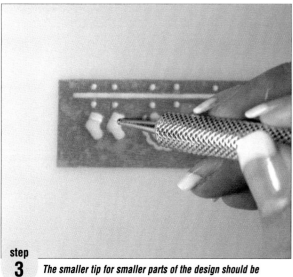

step 3
The smaller tip for smaller parts of the design should be embossed using the small end of the tip.

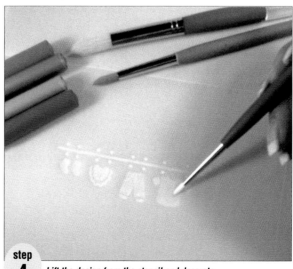

step 4
Lift the design from the stencil and decorate with paint, pens, inks or chalks.

ⓘ Dry-embossing produces a subtle but sophisticated appearance. A stylus raises the surface of the paper by burnishing a design on the paper using templates. Metal templates work the best, but you may also use the plastic ones designed for stencilling

Wedding by Sharon Kerr

Materials:
- ☐ white hammer cardstock
- ☐ white vellum
- ☐ sheer ribbon
- ☐ silver cord
- ☐ Making Memories eyelets
- ☐ 3D foam pads
- ☐ Lasting Impressions Heart template

To create:

1 Score and fold the white cardstock to create a card blank. Cut a rectangle approx 4.5x13.5cm, then cut a slightly smaller vellum rectangle.

2 Emboss the vellum using the heart designs.

3 Attach the vellum to the white rectangle with eyelets. Mount this onto the card blank with 3D pads.

4 Tie the ribbon and cord through the eyelets and tie in a bow.

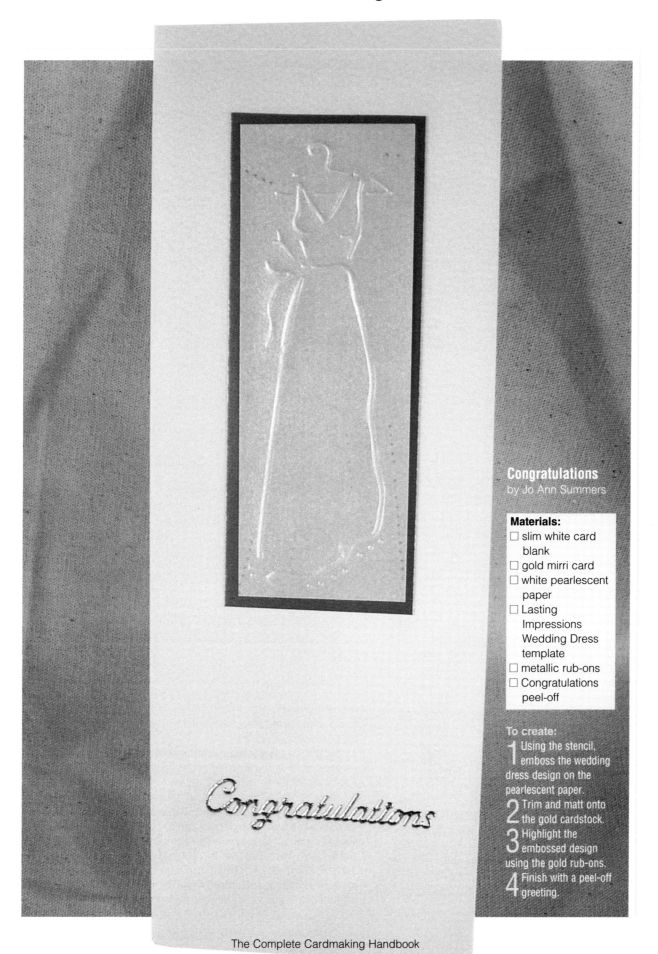

Congratulations
by Jo Ann Summers

Materials:
- [ ] slim white card blank
- [ ] gold mirri card
- [ ] white pearlescent paper
- [ ] Lasting Impressions Wedding Dress template
- [ ] metallic rub-ons
- [ ] Congratulations peel-off

To create:

1 Using the stencil, emboss the wedding dress design on the pearlescent paper.

2 Trim and matt onto the gold cardstock.

3 Highlight the embossed design using the gold rub-ons.

4 Finish with a peel-off greeting.

Turn in time by Natalie O'Shea

Materials:
- ☐ A4 beige cardstock
- ☐ K&Co script paper
- ☐ Hot Off The Press clock paper from the Ivory Sarabook collection
- ☐ 7gypsies script paper
- ☐ Lasting Impressions Wedding template

Wishes stencil:
- ☐ A4 beige cardstock
- ☐ Dreamweaver heart stencil (Lynell Harlow LM125)
- ☐ brown chalk inkpad
- ☐ Magic Scraps Virtual Metal foil adhesive sheet
- ☐ Making Memories spiral clip from The Scrapbookhouse

To create:

1. Attach the two brass stencils to the front of your metal foil with low-tack tape. Turn the metal over and, using an embossing tool, push the metal through the stencil. Once complete, remove the stencils, ensuring that you have pushed through every mark, and trim to leave an even border with deckle-edged scissors.

2. Remove the adhesive backing, stick to a rectangle of 7gypsies script paper and trim, leaving a 1cm border using deckle-edged scissors. Push a spiral paperclip onto the top-right corner.

3. Fold a piece of A4 beige card in half to make an A5 base card. Cut a rectangle of the K&Co script paper to just smaller than A5. Go around the edge with a brown chalk inkpad. Attach to the centre of your card. Cut a piece of the HOTP clock paper to the height of the K&Co script paper and approximately 10cm wide. Tear the right- and left-hand side to produce a feathered effect. Edge with brown chalk inkpad. Attach to the right-hand side of your card over the script paper. Attach the metal-embossed frame to the left-hand side of your base card using 3D foam tape.

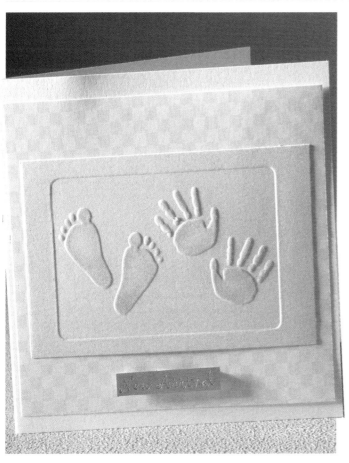

New Arrival by Natalie O'Shea

Materials:
- ☐ white cardstock
- ☐ Lasting Impressions patterned paper
- ☐ Lasting Impressions Senti-Metals metal messages
- ☐ pink ink
- ☐ small stencil brush
- ☐ American Traditional brass stencil - Erin, 2 weeks (FS-962)

To create:

1. Attach the stencil to plain pink paper with low-tack adhesive.
2. Using a ball tool, emboss the image through the stencil onto the paper. When finished, keep the stencil in place and use the pink ink and stencil brush to gently colour the image – leave a small area in the centre of each hand and foot plain to create dimension.
3. Remove the stencil and attach the plain pink paper to a larger piece of pink check paper. Stick this to the front of your white cardstock base card.
4. Attach the metal message to the card with 3D foam pads.

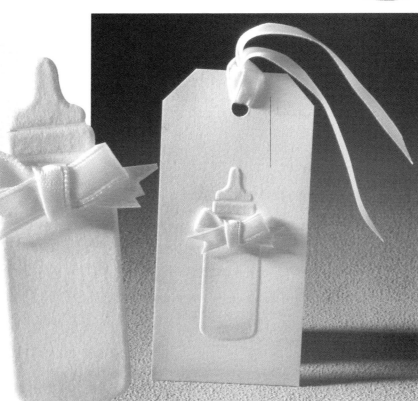

Pink Bottle Tag by Natalie O'Shea

Materials:
- ☐ white cardstock
- ☐ pink ink
- ☐ pink ribbon
- ☐ Lasting Impressions Bottle stencilstencil - Erin, 2 weeks (FS-962)

To create:

1. Cut a tag from some white cardstock. Attach the stencil to the tag with low-tack adhesive.
2. Using a ball tool, emboss the image through the stencil onto the card.
3. When finished, keep the stencil in place and use the pink ink and stencil brush to gently colour the image – leave a small area in the centre of the bottle plain to create dimension. Also colour around the edge of the tag.
4. Attach some pink satin ribbon around the tag hole and affix a small bow across the neck of the bottle.

Embossing

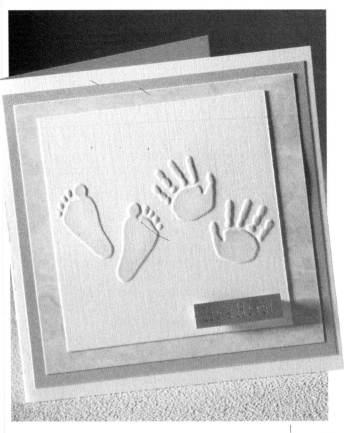

He is Here by Natalie O'Shea

Materials:
- ☐ white cardstock
- ☐ blue astro and marbled paper
- ☐ Lasting Impressions Senti-Metals metal messages
- ☐ blue ink
- ☐ small stencil brush
- ☐ American Traditional brass stencil - Erin, 2 weeks (FS-962)

To create:

1. Attach the stencil to plain white card with low-tack adhesive.
2. Using a ball tool, emboss the image through the stencil onto the card.
3. When finished, keep the stencil in place and use the blue ink and stencil brush to gently colour the image – leave a small area in the centre of each hand and foot plain to create dimension.
4. Mount this onto blue marble-patterned paper, then onto blue astro paper, then onto your card, leaving a narrow margin each time.
5. Using 3D foam pads, attach the silver metal message to the bottom right-hand corner of the card.

Blue Pram Tag

by Natalie O'Shea

Materials:
- ☐ cream astro card
- ☐ Lasting Impressions blue check patterned paper
- ☐ blue ink
- ☐ small stencil brush
- ☐ gold paper
- ☐ blue satin ribbon
- ☐ Lasting Impressions Pram stencil

To create:

1. Attach the stencil to some cream astro card with low-tack adhesive.
2. Using a ball tool, emboss the image through the stencil onto the card.
3. When finished, keep the stencil in place and use the blue ink and stencil brush to gently colour both the image and around the edges of the tag.
4. On a separate piece of blue check paper, emboss the pram hood and wheels. Cut them out, leaving a very narrow border. Attach them over the original embossed pattern with 3D foam pads.
5. Use a hole punch to add a touch of gold paper to the centre of the pram wheels.
6. Cover the top of the card with check paper, then edge this with decorative scissors. Finally, attach some blue satin ribbon through the tag hole.

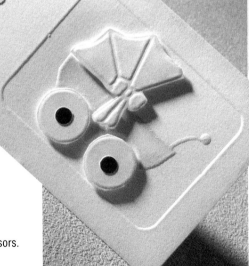

Embossing

I Do by Lousette Ashton

Materials:

☐ A6 folded card blank
☐ BasicGrey SweetPea Alyssa Blossom paper
☐ Bazzill Scrapworks Colours Orange Crush cardstock
☐ Kopp oval metal tag
☐ MAMBI Wedding rub-ons
☐ Lasting Impressions Wedding Cake embossing template
☐ ColorBox Chestnut Roan fluid chalk inkpad
☐ small white brads

To create:

1. Glue a strip of torn dark orange cardstock to the bottom of the card blank. Rub brown ink around the edges of the card.

2. Emboss the wedding cake design onto the pink patterned paper and lightly sand to reveal the white paper core. Add two small white brads as flower centres. Cut into a large tag shape.

3. Add the 'I do' rub-ons to the metal tag and glue to the paper tag, making sure the holes line up. Add some white ribbon and glue the completed tag to the card blank using 3D pads.

Embossing

Tools for the job

✿ cardstock or plasticard
✿ punch or die-cut shape
✿ embossing stylus
✿ card to emboss

Make your own stencils

Stencil embossing or dry embossing requires a stencil or template. Traditionally made from brass, these are used to shape the paper. However, a template can be made easily from a variety of materials

A cost-effective way of creating a stencil is with a medium thickness of cardstock or plasticard and a punch or die-cutting machine. The only thing to bear in mind with these types of templates are that they will not last as long as the purchased type due to the materials they are made from.

Punch from your card the chosen shape, et voila! You have a template. Punches and die-cut machines' designs are generally chunky, which means that the designs of stencil will follow suit. You could create a design and hand-cut it with a craft knife and glass mat, although this can be time consuming. Once you have created the stencil, emboss in the same way as you would normally.

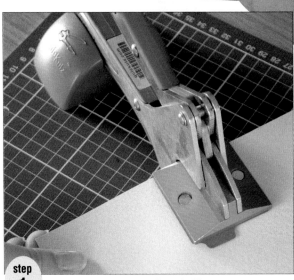

step 1 *Take your chosen shape or die, and with this cut your shape from cardstock.*

step 2 *Take the negative and trim to size – this is what you will use as the stencil. Keep the die shape as this could be used in another project.*

step 3 *Take the card that you want to emboss and place over the stencil, against a lightbox or a window, and emboss as normal.*

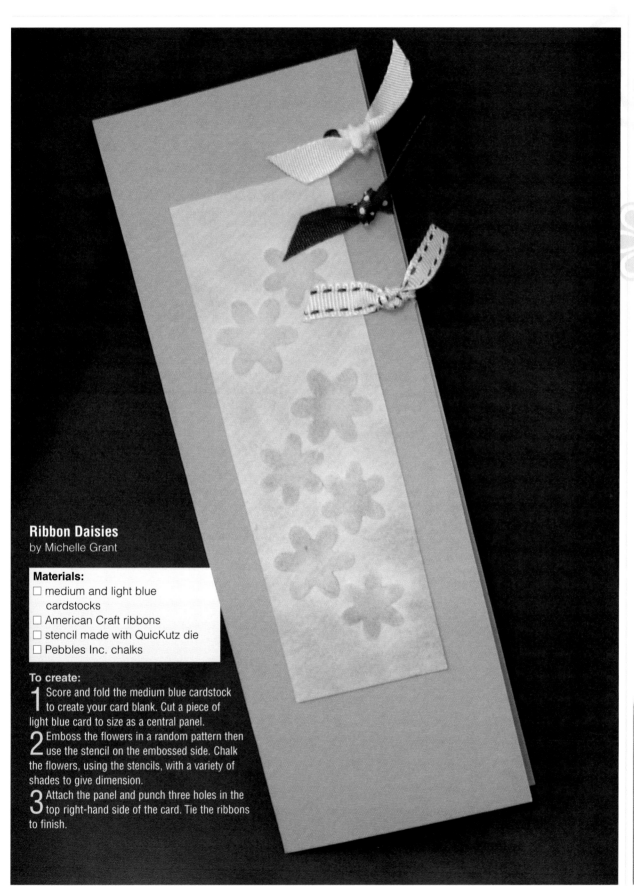

Ribbon Daisies
by Michelle Grant

Materials:
- ☐ medium and light blue cardstocks
- ☐ American Craft ribbons
- ☐ stencil made with QuicKutz die
- ☐ Pebbles Inc. chalks

To create:

1 Score and fold the medium blue cardstock to create your card blank. Cut a piece of light blue card to size as a central panel.

2 Emboss the flowers in a random pattern then use the stencil on the embossed side. Chalk the flowers, using the stencils, with a variety of shades to give dimension.

3 Attach the panel and punch three holes in the top right-hand side of the card. Tie the ribbons to finish.

Embossing

i A stencil is a letter, number, cartoon, typographical symbol, illustration, or any other shape or image in cutout form (it can be cut out of paper, cardboard, metal or other material). Stencils can be used to emboss as well as to create clean edges when the ink or chalks are added.

Tools for the job

✿ embossing stamp pad
✿ stamp
✿ embossing powder
✿ heat gun
✿ cardstock

Heat embossing

Embossing adds an elegant dimensional element to any stamped design. It may look difficult, but it is in fact one of the easiest and most effective rubber-stamping techniques of all

Materials:

☐ Craftwork Cards plain white, black and red card
☐ Hammered white card
☐ The Mulberry Bush yellow snow paper
☐ VersaColor black pigment inkpad
☐ Brilliance Pearlescent Jade pigment inkpad
☐ ColorBox Frost White pigment inkpad
☐ crystal embossing powder
☐ marker pens
☐ Diamond glitter glue
☐ mini gold brads
☐ Hero Arts C2356 Strawflower Daisy rubberstamp
☐ Elzybells Art Stamps 02.019.J Flower Background rubberstamp

he top secret to perfect heat embossing is to use a heat gun, a quality pigment embossing inkpad, deeply etched quality stamps and good cardstock. When adding embossing ink, you should dab or pat the inkpad onto the rubber surface, making sure that you give the stamp an even coverage.

When applying the stamp to the cardstock, make sure that you press down firmly. Don't rock the stamp, as this will blur the image. It can be easier to stamp when in a standing position. Make sure that you cover the design thoroughly with embossing powder immediately. Gently tap the excess powder from the cardstock rather than blowing on the paper, as the latter will loosen the powder and ruin the design. An even covering of embossing powder will add a beautiful shiny finish.

Daisy Trio
by Kay Carley

Make a hammered white top-folded landscape card to measure 10x21cm. Cut a white panel and a piece of 9x20cm snow paper, and cut a slightly larger black panel. Place the snow paper over the white panel, layer onto the black panel and then onto the card front. Secure all the layers using the mini brads by punching a hole in each corner, inserting a brad, then bending the prongs back on the inside of the card to secure.

Ink the Strawflower Daisy stamp with the black inkpad and stamp onto white card. Emboss with the crystal embossing powder. Repeat twice, then colour in all the images. Trim each image, leaving a narrow white border and layer onto slightly larger red panels.

Cut a white panel to measure 6.5x15cm. Ink the Flower Background stamp with the white inkpad and stamp onto the panel. Repeat until the panel is covered with flowers. Emboss with the crystal embossing powder. Using the sponge wedge and the Jade inkpad, apply ink onto the top half of the panel only, then layer onto a slightly larger black panel.

Mount the sponged panel centrally onto the card with 3D pads and mount each flower panel onto the sponged panel with 3D pads. Apply glitter glue to the centres of the flowers.

Stamping

step 1 *Ink the stamp with either an embossing inkpad or a slow-drying pigment inkpad by placing the stamp rubber-side up on your work surface and lightly patting the inkpad over the rubber design.*

step 2 *Once the stamp has been thoroughly inked, press it firmly onto the surface of the card.*

step 3 *Working over an A4 sheet of clean paper, pour embossing powder over the printed image.*

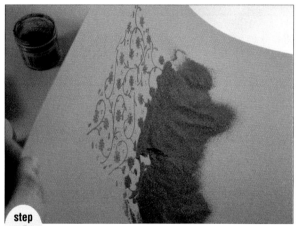

step 4 *Holding the card with the printed image, carefully tap off the excess powder. (The wet ink of the stamped image will retain the amount of powder it needs.)*

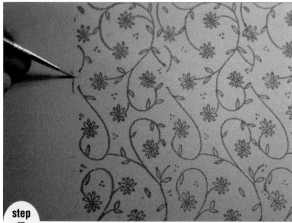

step 5 *Brush away any stray specks of embossing powder with a small, dry paintbrush. If this isn't done, the specks will be embossed too and could spoil the finished result. Return the excess embossing powder to the jar.*

step 6 *Heat the image with a heat tool, keeping the tool in one place and roughly 10cm away from the image. When the powder begins to melt, slowly move the tool across the image until all of it has melted and become embossed. The result is a raised shiny image.*

i **Embossing with heat is the way to create a raised design on paper, although it does not shape. When you heat the powder, it melts and creates a bond with the paper and ink**

Christmas Poinsetta
by Karen McGolderick

Materials:
☐ Dawn Bibby Designs Three Leaves & Large Flower stamps
☐ Hobby Art vertical greeting stamp
☐ PSX Christmas Montage Collection stamp
☐ cream card blank
☐ gold ribbon
☐ gold cord
☐ gold embossing powder
☐ small tag
☐ silicone glue

Cut a piece of gold mirror card as a backing panel. Stamp the image onto cream cardstock and attach the gold ribbon to the left-hand side.

Position the 'Best Wishes' peel-off in the centre of the tag. Tie gold cord around the tag, and glue the cord onto the ribbon. Attach the bow on top using silicone glue. Stamp the leaves onto cardstock and emboss, then cut out each one.

Stamp two flowers onto cardstock, emboss and cut out each one. Colour the leaves with your chosen glitter and attach to the card. Attach the poinsettia flower.

Secure the stamped montage image to the backing panel, then attach the backing panel to the card. Stamp the vertical 'Merry Christmas' greeting next to the panel and emboss.

Stamping

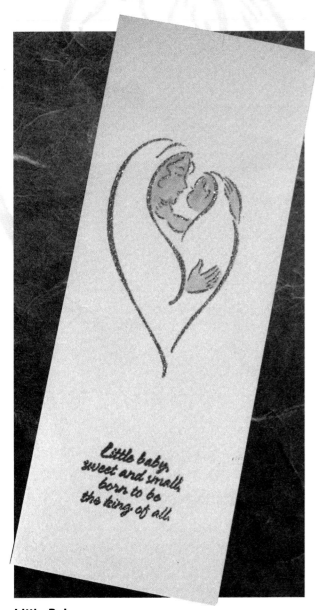

Tree
by Trish Latimer

Materials:
- ☐ cream cardstock
- ☐ brown cardstock
- ☐ handmade paper
- ☐ fibres
- ☐ clear embossing ink
- ☐ gold detail embossing powder
- ☐ tree stamp
- ☐ anti-static bag
- ☐ heat gun
- ☐ brown inks
- ☐ sponge dauber

Swipe an anti-static bag over a piece of torn-edged brown cardstock. This will prevent static causing the embossing powder to stick where you don't want it to.

Stamp the tree using clear embossing ink, and emboss with gold powder.

Matt onto a torn-edged handmade paper panel, and adhere to a cream card blank that has had the edges sponged with brown ink.

Add fibres to the brown panel.

Little Baby
by Mrs GA Gardner

Materials:
- ☐ Prism cardstocks
- ☐ Stampin' Up Baby stamp
- ☐ Funstamps message stamp
- ☐ ColorBox Quick Silver inkpad
- ☐ JudiKins silver embossing powder
- ☐ Tombow pens

Score and fold your card to create a card blank.

Stamp the designs with silver ink then emboss using the silver embossing powder.

Colour the hair, face and hands with the Tombow markers.

- ✿ stamps
- ✿ inkpads
- ✿ Post-it notes
- ✿ cardstock
- ✿ scissors/paper trimmer
- ✿ shaving brush
- ✿ sponge dauber

Masking

Give a stamp more versatility while adding greater depth to your stamping projects with the simple technique of masking

Masking is one of the most impressive stamping techniques. It adds depth and perspective to artwork by giving the effect of stamped images behind, coming out of, or going into each other. The technique of masking is simple, yet it will produce a professional-looking polish. You will soon be busy stamping armies of frogs, making animals peer round corners, filling baskets and jars with flowers or candy, or concocting crazy combinations of all of the above!

You start by stamping the image that you want to appear in the foreground onto your card or paper. Stamp the same image onto a Post-it note or piece of scrap paper then cut around it (very carefully) to form the mask. Position this over your original stamped design and stamp over it with the image that you would like to appear in the background. It can take a while to get your head around this, because usually you would begin from the back and work forward, tucking things behind one another as you go; with masking you do the opposite. But once you have for the hang of it, you will be surprised just how versatile your stamping will become.

The steps below and the Vintage Dressmaker card use the grid masking technique, whereas the Love and Oriental cards use the instructions outlined above.

The Vintage Dressmaker card
by Trish Latimer

Materials:
- ☐ C6 dark brown card
- ☐ cream cardstock
- ☐ 3M Post-it notes
- ☐ shaving brush
- ☐ sponge dauber
- ☐ double-sided tape
- ☐ buckle embellishment & ribbon
- ☐ Kars decorative crystal topaz beadstone
- ☐ Diamond Glaze
- ☐ Artistic Wire Co wire
- ☐ PVA glue
- ☐ Brilliance Galaxy Gold & Tiramisu inks
- ☐ VersaFine Vintage Sepia inkpad
- ☐ Hero Arts G2675 Vintage Button Collage & F2674 Long Writing background stamps
- ☐ Beeswax 685R cracked background stamp
- ☐ Stampington & Co S7115 Nostalgia cube & S7114 Notions-fourX by Maureen Blackman stamps

Trim a section of cream cardstock to 14x9.5cm and create the grid as shown on p53. Use Brilliance Galaxy Gold ink for the cracked background stamp, the Tiramisu for the stippling and sponging, and the Vintage Sepia to stamp the main image.

Thread ribbon through the buckle embellishment and secure the ends to the back of the finished gridded card with double-sided tape.

Attach the gridded card to the brown cardstock with double-sided tape.

Thread the beadstone onto two lengths of wire, then twist to secure. Tie a double knot in a length of ribbon. Wrap the wire around the knot, then affix to the cardstock using Diamond Glaze or PVA. Weigh down under a heavy book while it dries.

Stamping

step 1 *Start with a 9.5x14cm piece of card. This is the perfect size to mount onto a C6 card. Using a shaving brush, gently stipple a background with the ink of your choice. It's also a nice touch to over-stamp with a decorative background stamp for added interest.*

step 2 *Select one of your stamps to create the main image, and impress this slightly off-centre in the middle of the card.*

step 3 *Using large Post-its, mask a line along an edge of the image. If your image doesn't have a readymade frame, create one by placing a Post-it under, over or to the side of your image. Stipple along the line of the Post-it with a shaving brush, then sponge along it with a sponge dauber.*

step 4 *Remove the Post-it, then repeat step 3 along all sides of your image. You may need two Post-its for the longer edges. When you have created the masked frames for all sides of the central image, you will have eight clearly defined areas arranged in a grid.*

step 5 *Mask off one area of the grid at a time, using the grid lines as a guide for laying down the Post-its. Stamp an image into the space you have exposed on your cardstock. For the best results, use a stamp that fills the space, or repeatedly stamp the space using a smaller stamp.*

step 6 *Stamp one area at a time, re-masking where necessary. The example here is almost finished, with just three areas remaining to be stamped. Once you have filled in all the blanks, mount the grid and embellish according to the theme you have created with the images.*

Masking is the technique of covering a stamped image so that other images may be placed partly over it without the overlapping area being visible

Oriental Faux Postage
by Trish Latimer

Materials:
- ☐ black cardstock
- ☐ Oriental background papers
- ☐ tassel
- ☐ Oriental coin
- ☐ gold thread
- ☐ Faux Postage paper
- ☐ thin masking tape
- ☐ red, orange, yellow & black pigment inks
- ☐ mixture of small Oriental stamps

To create:

1. Using thin masking tape, mask off four sections of Faux Postage paper, as shown. Sponge red, yellow and orange pigment ink into the rectangles exposed by the tape.

2. Stamp various Oriental images on top of the red/yellow/orange colour using black ink. Remove the tape to expose the stamp shapes.

3. Matt onto black cardstock then adhere to a black card blank that has been decorated with Oriental background papers. Add a tassel and a threaded Oriental coin.

Love
by Jemma White

Materials:
- ☐ cream cardstock
- ☐ red & brown inkpads
- ☐ red handmade paper
- ☐ gold embossing powder
- ☐ stamps
- ☐ Big and Bossy inkpad

To create:

1. Score and fold your cardstock to make a card blank, and mask the front of the card with two pieces of torn paper.

2. In the masked area, apply the word stamps using the red inks. Colour the area with the brown ink using the direct-to-paper technique.

3. Cut a heart shape from scrap cardstock, cover it in clear embossing ink then cover with gold embossing powder.

4. Heat the embossing powder. Once it has melted and whilst it is still hot, stamp into it. Mount onto handmade paper and feather the edges. Adhere to the card.

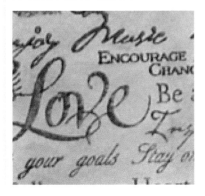

The Gardener's Notebook
by Trish Latimer

Materials:
- □ white cardstock
- □ sponge dauber
- □ 3M Post-it notes
- □ shaving brush
- □ matt board
- □ white Reflex paper
- □ hole punch
- □ hammer
- □ eyelet setter & gold eyelets
- □ embossing tool/bone scorer
- □ fibres
- □ Krylon gold pen
- □ double-sided tape
- □ VersaMagic Niagra Mist ink
- □ Brilliance Galaxy Gold ink
- □ VersaColor Bamboo, Split Pea, Misty, Mauve, Canary, Heliotrope, Raspberry & Boysenberry inkpads
- □ Hampton Art DF2240 Splatter stamp
- □ Hero Arts Real Flower series F3269, F2663, F2665, F3255, D2910 & H3258 stamps

Use your PC to create the text, print it onto white Reflex paper, then attach it to 5x5cm of matt board. Sponge the edges using a dauber and the Niagra Mist then, using the splatter stamp and Galaxy Gold ink, over-stamp the sponged edges. Finish off the edges of the matt board with the gold Krylon pen. Use the square as a guide for the perimeter of the gridding section on the card. Trace the outline onto the cardstock. Set the square aside to be attached when finishing.

Mask and sponge the grid as shown on p53, using the Splatter stamp and Niagra Mist ink to create the stippled background. Stamp the floral images using the VersaColors, blending different colours on the one stamp to create a watercolour effect.

Measure 2cm down from the top of the cardstock and score a horizontal line. Fold the card and crease using the bone folder. Measure another line 2.5cm down from the top of the cardstock and fold.

Cut a stack of white copy paper to a depth of 0.5cm, measuring 10x14cm. Place the copy paper on top of the 10x14cm matt board for the inside and back cover of the notebook. Use an eyelet punch and hammer to punch three holes through the paper and board.

Position the front cover over the paper and matt board, folding it over the top and back. This will enable you to mark the placement for the holes, so that they align with the binding holes. Remove the front cover and punch three holes, then set a gold eyelet in each opening.

You're ready to assemble! Use double-sided tape to attach the small 2cm-wide section of the cover fold over the back of the notebook to the matt board. You will then need to punch through the three openings again to create openings in the tape.

Place the stack of copy paper in between the front and back cover and line up all of the holes. Thread the fibres through each of the openings and tie a secure knot at the top of the notebook to create the bound finish and a textured touch.

Finally, place and attach the central image matt board design you first created to the front of the notebook.

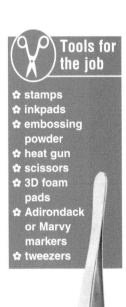

Tools for the job

- ✿ stamps
- ✿ inkpads
- ✿ embossing powder
- ✿ heat gun
- ✿ scissors
- ✿ 3D foam pads
- ✿ Adirondack or Marvy markers
- ✿ tweezers

Dimensional stamping

Decoupage is another technique that we have inherited from the Netherlands. Adapted from using printed sheets of paper to using stamped images, it's the perfect way to get your stamped image to lift out from the card

Many stamps are suitable for this technique, and there are specialist ones designed specifically for it, such as medallion stamps. Decoupage simply involves stamping a number of copies of one image, then selecting elements of that image to be cut out and raised up, getting smaller as you get nearer the front. Heat embossing works well with this, as the edges of the design become more defined and are easier to cut around.

Once you have selected the elements that are going to form the design, you can colour them with markers such as the Adirondack or Marvy Le Plume pens. The elements can then be built up onto your card using Pop Dots or 3D foam pads. If the design is particularly intricate, like the medallion stamps featured here, you may choose to use a silicone gel glue applied with a cocktail stick.

Teddy on a Stool
by Gina Martin

Materials:
- ☐ white hammer card
- ☐ smooth white card
- ☐ silicone glue
- ☐ cocktail stick
- ☐ Marvey le Plume II Rosewood & Steel Blue pens
- ☐ brown crystal lacquer
- ☐ Chatterbox Den paper
- ☐ Hobbyart I Didn't Do It stamp

Colour your stamp with the Rosewood pen, stamp the image onto the white card and repeat five times. Colour all of the bears with the Rosewood pen and their scarves with the blue. Cut out the first image and colour the stool with the brown crystal lacquer. Cut out the next layer, removing the back bar off the stool, and colour the stool again. Leave to dry.

For the next layer, cut out the bear only. Then cut out the scarf and forearm. Lastly, cut out the smallest part that is the hanging piece of the scarf. When the lacquer is dry, begin to assemble the picture. Use the glue and the cocktail stick to attach the second layer to the original picture. Then glue the whole bear on top of the second one. Glue the scarf and arm to the bear and lastly add the piece of scarf. Leave to dry.

Fold the white hammer card to C6 size. Cut a diagonal piece of the patterned paper and attach to the bottom-left corner of the card. Attach the decoupage bear to the centre of the card. Make a greeting for the top, using either a stamp or your computer, and attach.

step 1 *Stamp the image four times onto white card with embossing ink and heat-emboss with black powder. Using a fine-tipped glue bottle, apply glue to the outer borders of one of the images (layer 1), sprinkle the glitter on and shake off any excess. Set aside to dry.*

step 2 *Take another one of the stamped images, apply glue to the outer border of this layer (layer 2), and glitter in the same way. Take the third and fourth stamped images and repeat the glitter process for layers 3 and 4 until the required areas of each layer are covered, then allow the four pieces to dry.*

Stamping

Sitting Comfortably
by Gina Martin

Materials:
- ☐ white hammer card
- ☐ white plain card
- ☐ silicone glue
- ☐ cocktail stick
- ☐ Paper Adventures Orchid plaid patterned paper
- ☐ Rubbadubbadoo Animals On Sofa stamp
- ☐ Stick 'n' Stamp letters
- ☐ Marvey le Plume II Burnt Umber, Black, Grey, Rosewood, Violet, Terracotta, Yellow & Wisteria pens
- ☐ black inkpad
- ☐ clear embossing powder
- ☐ Art Impressions A2054 blossoms

Stamp out three images of the sofa stamp using the black ink. Cover with clear embossing powder, remove the excess powder, and heat using a heat tool.

Colour the sofa with the Wisteria pen, then colour one flower on the blossoms stamp with the violet pen and decorate the sofa. Colour the dog using the Burnt Umber pen, the nose of the dog and the rabbit using the black pen, the rabbit with the grey pen, the bird with the yellow, and the cat using the black and terracotta pens. Colour all of the animals on all three of the images.

Cut out the rabbit's, cat's and bird's heads and glue these to the first picture using the silicone glue. Cut out the dog, leaving out his back legs, and glue him to the first picture. Cut out the dog's head and front feet and glue them onto the second layer.

Cut out the front and arms of the sofa in one piece and attach to the first layer. Then cut out the bottom of the sofa and the arms, and attach to the second layer. Leave to dry.

Make your base card using the white hammer card.

Attach some of the patterned paper to the centre, leaving an even border on all sides. Use the Stick 'n' Stamp letters to stamp your greeting, colouring with the violet pen. Attach your sofa to the bottom centre of your base card.

step 3 Cut a piece of silver pearlescent paper and attach to the centre of the card. Cut a piece of black card and attach to the centre of the silver paper. Cut a piece of silver pearlescent paper and attach to the centre of the black card. Attach a thin silver peel-off border to the centre of the black card border and trim with a craft knife.

step 4 Once all the glittered areas have dried, cut out each layer and stick them over one other using 3D foam pads. Attach the complete image to the top centre of the final silver pearlescent paper strip. Attach the peel-off sentiment to the bottom centre of the silver pearlescent strip.

i Decoupage is the art of cutting out elements of a design and building a three-dimensional picture from those elements

Get Well Soon
by Clair Simmons

Materials:
- ☐ silver pearlescent paper
- ☐ black card
- ☐ white vellum
- ☐ Creative Stamping Medallion HH 1003F stamp
- ☐ The Art Institute black monochromatic glitter & clear glitter glue
- ☐ 'Get Well Soon' peel-offs
- ☐ Stampendous detail white and detail silver embossing powders
- ☐ embossing inkpad
- ☐ double-sided tape

To create:

1 Stamp the image from HH 1003 F onto white vellum four times using the embossing inkpad. Heat-emboss two with detail silver and two with detail white embossing powder.

2 Carefully cut around the outer edge of one of the silver images and the edge of the third layer.

3 Carefully cut around the edge of the second and fourth white images.

4 Cut a piece of silver pearlescent paper and attach to the top centre of the card blank. Cut a piece of black card. Attach the black card to the centre of the silver pearlescent paper.

5 Apply a small amount of glitter glue in the centre on the back of each of the images and layer on top of each other. Then attach to the centre of the black card.

6 Attach the peel-off sentiment to the bottom half of the card.

Thinking of You
by Clair Simmons

Materials:
- ☐ silver pearlescent paper
- ☐ white and black card
- ☐ Creative Stamping Medallion HH 1003 F stamp
- ☐ The Art Institute silver glitter & clear glitter glue
- ☐ 'Thinking of You' and corner peel-off stickers
- ☐ Stampendous detail white embossing powder
- ☐ embossing inkpad
- ☐ 3D foam pads
- ☐ double-sided tape

To create:

1. Stamp the image from HH 1003 F four times onto black card with embossing ink, and heat-emboss with the white powder. Using a fine-tipped glue bottle, apply glue to the selected areas to be glittered on layer 1. Sprinkle the glitter on and shake off any excess. Then set aside to dry. Do the same to layers 2–4 and set them aside to dry.

2. Cut a piece of silver pearlescent paper and attach to the centre top half of the card. Cut a piece of black card slightly smaller and attach to the centre of the silver paper. Cut a piece of silver pearlescent paper, again, slightly smaller, and attach to the centre of the black card.

3. Attach a silver corner peel-off sticker to the bottom right-hand corner.

4. Once all the glittered areas have dried, cut out each layer and attach them over each other using 3D foam pads.

5. Attach the complete image to the centre of the final silver pearlescent paper.

6. Attach the peel-off sentiment to the bottom centre of the silver pearlescent strip.

Because a large part of the work in decoupage is in cutting out, it is most important to use a sharp cutting instrument. This will ensure that you get clean edges and precise cuts

Stamping

Tools for the job

✿ variety of stamps
✿ Sea Shells, Sea Brights & Adirondack inkpads
✿ water spritzer
✿ watercolour paper
✿ heat tool

Brushless watercolour

With a little bit of magic – and some ink – it's possible to turn a simple stamp into a beautiful watercolour painting

The brushless watercolour technique is used by a variety of crafters. It is best suited to stamps that are floral or of a brushstroke design. Hero Arts has a beautiful range of foliage stamps that are perfect for this technique, or you could make a good start with Sea Shells, Sea Brights and Adirondack dye inkpads. Colour is applied directly onto the rubberstamp with the edges of the inkpad. You don't need to worry about inks getting mixed on the pad if you start with the lightest colour first, and the chances of contaminating the pad are small anyway.

Once the colours have been added to the correct areas of the stamp, the surface of the stamp needs to be spritzed once or twice with the magic: water. Do not over-wet the ink and stamp, or you'll end up with an inky muddy mess! Once the water has been applied, immediately stamp the image onto watercolour paper – standard paper won't give the same textured finish. The reason that these inkpads work so well is that they are water based. You should heat-set the image to prevent the design from bleeding too much. This can be done with a heat gun.

In all, this is an easy technique that is visually stunning – it looks like a proper watercolour painting, but you don't need to be an artist to achieve it.

Thinking of You
by Michelle Grant

Materials:
☐ brown and green Adirondack inkpads
☐ Hero Arts stamps
☐ white card blank
☐ Making Memories magnetic letter stamps

Ink up the fir tree stamp and wet with each stamp, but don't re-ink.
Stamp the title on the bottom of the card.

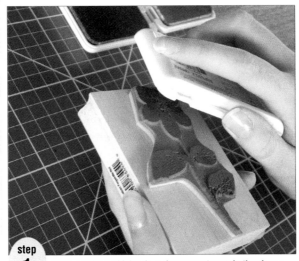

step 1 *Using a palette of inkpads, colour your stamps in the chosen design. Start by taking the lightest colour first and work up to the darkest.*

step 2 *Once complete, spray once or twice with a fine-mist water spritzer, being careful not to over-wet the stamp as this will make the inks run into each other.*

Stamping

Stamping

Family
by Michelle Grant

Materials:
- ☐ Chatterbox chipboard tags
- ☐ white card blank
- ☐ Making Memories blossoms
- ☐ Junkitz Long Brads by Tim Holtz
- ☐ Hero Arts Family stamp
- ☐ Sirus Hobby Script stamp
- ☐ American Craft ribbon
- ☐ black Adirondack inkpad
- ☐ black archival inkpad

Stamp the script background in black Adirondack ink and heat-set. Stamp the word family onto the chipboard tag.

Attach a blossom together using a brad and adhere to the tag. Tie a ribbon through the hole in the tag. Adhere the tag to the card.

step 3 *Stamp the image onto the watercolour paper. This must be done straightaway or the inks will run off the stamp. Heat-set the image if desired.*

Watercolour is a painting technique making use of water-soluble pigments that are either transparent or opaque and are formulated to bond the pigment to the paper. Although various mediums are used to paint upon, the most common is paper. Others include papyrus, bark papers, plastics, leather, fabric, wood and canvas

Happiness
by Michelle Grant

Materials:
- [ ] Chatterbox chipboard tags
- [ ] card blank
- [ ] Sea Shells, Sea Bright & Adirondack inkpads
- [ ] blank archival inkpad
- [ ] Hero Arts stamps

To create:

1. Colour your image of the flower using the inkpads, beginning with the lightest colour first, working up to the darkest. Once you have coloured the stamp, spritz it two or three times with water.

2. Stamp onto the card blank and heat-set with a heat tool. Tear along one edge and ink with the co-ordinating inkpads. Spritz the edge of this then heat-set again.

3. Finish with the title stamp in black archival ink.

Birthday Spots
by Michelle Grant

Materials:
- [ ] Hero Arts stamps
- [ ] white card blank
- [ ] Manila tag
- [ ] Adirondack inkpads in complementary colours
- [ ] Anita's greetings stamp
- [ ] Sea Shells, Sea Bright & Adirondack inkpads
- [ ] blank archival inkpad
- [ ] American Craft ribbon
- [ ] Adirondack markers
- [ ] orange handmade paper

To create:

1. Using the watercolour technique, stamp over the tag with the spotty stamp, beginning with the lightest colour and working up to the darkest.

2. Stamp the greeting using the archival ink and stamp an extra one on a scrap of white card. Mount this onto orange handmade paper and colour the details with Adirondack markers.

3. Thread the ribbon and attach the elements to the card.

Stamping

Stamping

Christmas Tree
by Michelle Grant

Materials:
- ☐ Prism green and white cardstocks
- ☐ Creative Stamping stamps
- ☐ Peeled Paint Distress inkpad
- ☐ Adirondack inkpad
- ☐ Ranger gold embossing powder
- ☐ American Craft ribbon
- ☐ 3D foam pads

Using the watercolour stamping technique, stamp the tree with the Adirondack inkpad. Heat-set the watercolour then, using an embossing pen, highlight the stars on the trees and heat-emboss them with gold embossing powder.

Cut out around the stamped image, ink the edges with distress ink and, using a piece of craft foam, apply the ink in a stippled way across the tree.

Score and fold the green card and attach the tree with 3D foam pads. Tie a bow and attach it to the front.

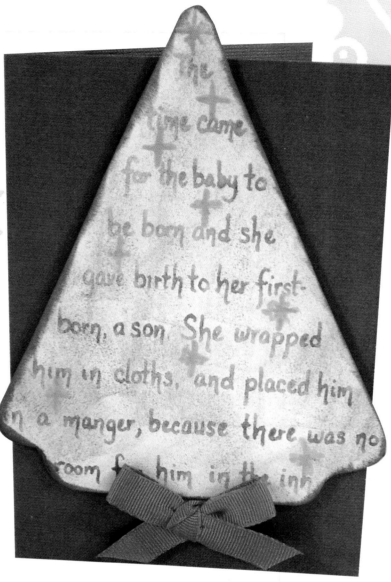

Happy Birthday
by Michelle Grant

Materials:
- ☐ card blank
- ☐ handmade paper
- ☐ Hero Arts stamps
- ☐ American Craft ribbon

Stamp the flower image three times onto the handmade paper, spritzing between stamps.

Tear the edges of the paper and adhere to the front of the card.

Stamp Happy Birthday on the ribbon and adhere to the front.

Tools for the job

❀ VersaMark inkpad
❀ UTEE or Chunky Embossing Crystals
❀ heat embossing tool
❀ stamps

Stamping into UTEE

Metal is big in papercrafts, and Ultra Thick Embossing Enamel combined with stamping provides a good way of cheating your way to getting the look

Stamping into UTEE is a technique for which you use ultra-thick embossing enamel or other similar product, create an embossed puddle, and then stamp into it while it is still hot. It does require practice before it's mastered, but once you get the hang of this technique you can create some gorgeous embellishments that cost very little when compared to the price you'd pay for the true metal equivalent.

Laugh
by Christi Snow

Be careful! UTEE gets extremely hot as you build layers. Do not touch until cool

Materials:
☐ VersaMark Watermark stamp pad
☐ Stamporium Plate #67 stamp sheet
☐ Impress Lavender dye-based inkpad
☐ Chunky Embossing Crystals Mink Lustre
☐ sei Kate Mini Memories assortment papers
☐ Dress It Up button
☐ PSX Pixie Affirmations
☐ eyelash fibre
☐ white card

To create:

1 Using the stamping into UTEE technique featured opposite, create the purse embellishment. Trim to size and mount onto a piece of green card then white card from the paper assortment.

2 Cut a card top also from the card assortment and mount onto a white card base.

3 Stamp 'Laugh' onto a scrap of white card and mount onto a scrap of green then purple card.

4 Next, wrap the eyelash fibre several times around the card.

5 Assemble using the example as your guide, and finishing off with a button offset from the 'Laugh' block.

UTEE

step 1
The first step in this process is to create a base for your stamping. A VersaMark watermark inkpad is ideal for this. Take a scrap piece of card and ink it completely with the VersaMark. You can do this easily by setting the card.

step 2
Next you need to sprinkle embossing enamel on top – try Suze Weinberg's Ultra Thick Embossing Enamel or a product made in the UK called Chunky Embossing Crystals, which works brilliantly. Alternatively, use several layers built up of normal embossing powder.

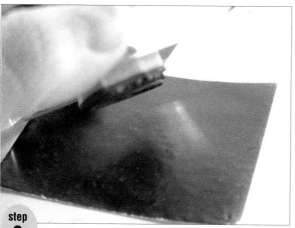

step 3
The tricky part is keeping your melted powder hot enough to stamp into for a good overall impression. Using a Melting Pot helps, but practice is the key to finding a system that works for you. If you don't get a good impression on your first try, just re-melt it and try again.

step 4
When heating, it works best if you do so from below. This keeps any loose particles of embossing powder from flying all over your workspace and also helps you maintain control over the melting process.

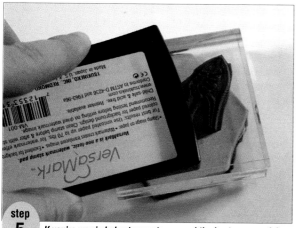

step 5
If you're worried about your stamps and the heat, you can ink them up with an additional layer of VersaMark to protect them and to help their release from the embossing, but this is not necessary.

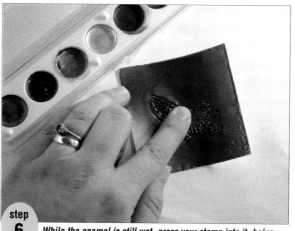

step 6
While the enamel is still wet, press your stamp into it, being sure to create an even impression. Complete the look by using rub-ons, chalks or other decorative mediums to completely customise your embellishment.

i Ultra Thick Embossing Enamel (UTEE) is a specially formulated, large-particle embossing powder. It can be used in the same way as ordinary embossing powders or can be used in melt art. UTEE comes in six colours: Clear, Gold, Bronze, Platinum, Black and Interference Blue. For a fabulous effect, mix and match all six!

UTEE

If the Shoe Fits
by Christi Snow

Materials:
- ☐ VersaMark Watermark stamp pad
- ☐ Stamporium Plate #67 stamp sheet
- ☐ Chunky Embossing Crystals Mink Lustre
- ☐ sei Kate Mini Memories assortment papers
- ☐ Dress It Up button
- ☐ eyelash fibre
- ☐ white card

1 Using the stamping into UTEE technique on page 65, create the shoe embellishment. Trim to size and mount this onto a piece of pink card then white card from the paper assortment.

2 Trim a piece of the circles paper from the paper assortment and mount onto a pink card base.

3 Trim a piece of the geometric paper from the paper assortment and mount onto white card, leaving a narrow border showing.

4 Assemble the card using the picture below as your guide.

5 Wrap the eyelash fibre around the spine of the card.

6 Finish off the card with three buttons adhered in a line in the lower-right corner.

The Colours of a Rose
by Christi Snow

Materials:
- ☐ VersaMark Watermark stamp pad
- ☐ Stamporium Plate #86 & #67 stamp sheets
- ☐ Impress Lavender dye-based inkpad
- ☐ Cloisonne sterling silver high-gloss granules
- ☐ Chunky Embossing Crystals Rose Gold Sparkle
- ☐ sei Kate Mini Memories assortment papers
- ☐ Making Memories upholstery brads
- ☐ ribbon, blossom & ribbon charm
- ☐ white card
- ☐ decorative scissors

To create:

1 Using the stamping into UTEE technique, create the French saying embellishment. To achieve the two-coloured look, first sprinkle the silver embossing powder in the centre, then the pink around the edges. Heat as normal and tear the embossed piece to size.

2 Trim a piece of the striped paper from the paper assortment and mount onto a purple card base.

3 Randomly stamp a piece of scrap white card with the swirl stamp and the lavender ink. Trim this with a pair of decorative scissors and mount onto a scrap of purple card with a small border showing at the top.

4 Wrap ribbon with a ribbon charm around the bottom border and attach to the card base.

5 Secure the embossed words to the front of the card with three brads.

6 Finish with a blossom and brad in the lower left of the card.

If your image does not stamp perfectly first time just reheat your UTEE and stamp again

UTEE

Materials:

- ☐ green and gold cardstocks
- ☐ 3 squares of mat board
- ☐ gold thread/eyelets
- ☐ clear embossing inkpad
- ☐ UTEE
- ☐ 3 shades of green embossing powder
- ☐ heat gun
- ☐ spiral stamp

To create:

1. Cover each square of mat board with embossing ink and sprinkle with UTEE. Repeat. For the third layer, use a normal green embossing powder.

2. Whilst the powder is still hot, press the spiral stamp into it. Adhere the three squares to a gold then green mat. Attach a torn-edged panel to a green card blank and add eyelets.

3. Weave gold thread through the eyelets. Adhere the panel containing the three squares to the card blank, using the example as a guide.

Green Spirals
by Trish Latimer

UTEE

Tools for the job

✿ Melting Pot/heat tool
✿ UTEE
✿ Teflon tweezers
✿ non-stick craft mat

Dipping into UTEE

If you want to give your projects the enamelled look, UTEE is the perfect weapon. It can be used in a variety of ways to turn paper or card embellishments into shiny, glass-like decorations

UTEE heats to exceptionally hot temperatures, so you need to take care when melting it. Using a heatproof and non-stick mat (like the Ranger craft mat) and Teflon tweezers is the way to go. This will reduce the chances of burning you or the surface that you are working on. You can use UTEE on any surface that won't melt with heat, for example: cardstock, wood, chipboard, mat board and cardboard.

Here are some of the effects that can be achieved by dipping into UTEE:

Wet look Apply adhesive and one layer of clear UTEE. Heat. The surface will be uneven and bumpy and will look wet. This look can be emphasised with the use of Pearl Ex or metallic rub-ons.

Glaze *(see Cute Bug & In the Pink cards)* Heat up your UTEE following the instructions with the Melting Pot and, holding your item with a pair of old tweezers, dip into the UTEE. You can dip the entire item or just parts of it.

Hold the item over the pan for a few seconds, as it will drip. Repeat until the surface becomes thick and smooth. This is a great way of adding dimension to punchies and pre-printed die-cuts.

Cracked-glass look *(see steps below and cards by Christi Snow)* Use the same method as for adding a glaze, but after the fourth layer, pop your piece into the freezer for about 15 minutes. Take it out and gently twist and bend it until the UTEE cracks. Tip: if you don't like the way it cracks you can reheat it until it smoothes out then refreeze it to try again.

Embedding items Use the glaze method. While two to three layers are still hot, push items into the UTEE. After embedding, add another layer if you choose. You can embed beads, wire, glitter, confetti, punchies, fibres, micro beads, paperclips, Pearl Ex – whatever you can think of!

3D items Pour hot UTEE into a mould

Cracked Glass Technique

step 1 *Stamp your image, and do all the colouring/decorating you intend to do. Trim to desired size. Apply VersaMark/embossing ink over the entire piece of card.*

step 2 *Pour on a generous amount of embossing powder, covering the card.*

UTEE

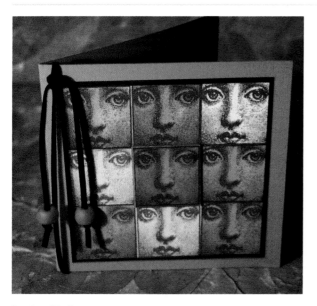

In the Pink
by Trish latimer

Materials:
- ☐ white, pink and black cardstock
- ☐ mat board
- ☐ pigment ink in shades of pink/purple
- ☐ black pigment ink
- ☐ face stamp
- ☐ UTEE
- ☐ clear embossing ink pad
- ☐ heat gun
- ☐ black cord
- ☐ pink beads

To create:

1 Colour white cardstock with eight different shades of pink/ purple ink, in a square pattern as shown. Over-stamp the face eight times on top of the coloured squares.

2 Colour a square of mat board with pink ink, and over-stamp with the face stamp. When dry, ink the whole square with clear embossing ink, and sprinkle on a layer of UTEE. Melt with the heat gun, then repeat twice more.

3 Three layers of UTEE will give a smooth, glass-like finish. Mount the tile onto the centre of the squares. Matt the whole panel onto black cardstock, and adhere to a pink card blank. Add a beaded black cord to the spine.

ⓘ A Melting Pot is a non-stick pan that has optimum temperature controls and large handles for pouring and lifting. You can melt, dip and pour UTEE, embossing powders, soap, candle wax, glue, candy and more

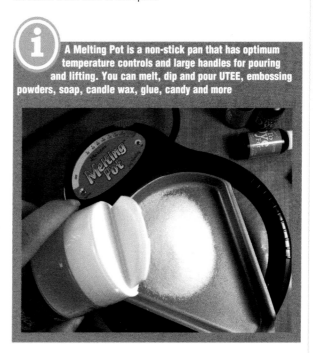

step 3 *Heat with your embossing gun from underneath (this helps to keep the powder from flying off), or in your Melting Pot. While the powder is still hot, pour more over it. Repeat this step between three to five times if you are using normal embossing powder. If you are using the ultra-thick, you only need to do one or two layers. Don't allow your powder to cool off between layers.*

step 4 *Immediately place the item into the freezer for approximately 10 minutes. When you pull it out, bend it slightly and it will develop hairline cracks. You only have about 15 seconds to do this before your hands heat up the piece too much for it to crack further. If you need to, place it back in the freezer and continue cracking until you are satisfied with the results.*

💡 Use different project pans for the different mediums that you melt in the pot. This way you will not have to waste what you don't use, you can just allow it to cool and keep it in the pan ready to pop in next time

UTEE

Don't panic when you dip your die-cut if bubbles form – this is normal and they will disappear as the UTEE cools

Cute Bug
by Katie Shanahan-Jones

Materials:
- ☐ Prismatics cardstock
- ☐ May Arts ribbons
- ☐ clear UTEE
- ☐ Melting Pot
- ☐ non-stick craft sheet
- ☐ QuickKutz Ladybird die
- ☐ Hero Arts Alpha stamps
- ☐ Making Memories blossoms
- ☐ Making Memories mini brads

To create:

1 Cut the body of the ladybird from black cardstock and the wings from red, and stick together.

2 Heat the clear UTEE in the Melting Pot and, holding the ladybird in tweezers, carefully slide it into the UTEE. Once completely coated, remove and place on a heatproof, non-stick craft mat to cool.

3 Once cool, trim any excess UTEE from the die with scissors. Mount onto your card as shown.

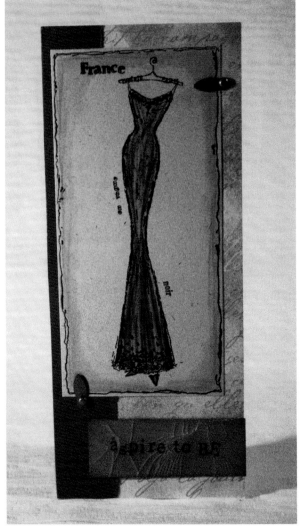

Aspire to Be
by Christi Snow

Materials:
- ☐ Stamps Happen Inc Vogue Silhouette stamp
- ☐ Inkadinkado Aspire to Be stamp
- ☐ StäzOn Jet Black inkpad
- ☐ Derwent watercolour pencils
- ☐ VersaMark Watermark inkpad and pen
- ☐ Making Memories Gold Photo Splits
- ☐ Sonnets French Poetry Print patterned paper
- ☐ UTEE clear
- ☐ violet and natural cardstock

To create:

1 Apply both stamps using black ink onto natural cardstock.

2 For the dress, colour with watercolour pencils. For the saying, create a layer of VersaMark and UTEE.

3 Immediately freeze and then shatter. Complete the assembly of the card.

UTEE

Fancy Dragonfly
by Christi Snow

Materials:
- ☐ lilac, olive green, cream and navy card
- ☐ Non Sequitor Stamps On Gossamer Wings from Blade Rubber
- ☐ VersaMark inkpad
- ☐ Pretty Petunia VersaMagic chalk pad
- ☐ Suze Weinberg's UltraThick Embossing Enamel (Gold) from Scraptastic
- ☐ fine gold embossing powder
- ☐ Pearl Ex Watercolour Palette from Artbase

To create:

1 On two scraps of navy card, stamp the swirl stamp using the VersaMark inkpad and fine gold embossing powder. Trim to size.

2 On a 6cm square piece of cream card, emboss using the gold UTEE. While it is still wet, impress the Dragonfly stamp into it. Freeze as normal for the shattered glass technique. Mount onto a piece of navy card, so that you have a small border all the way around, and then mount onto a 7.5cm square of the olive green card.

3 Cut a piece of the lilac card to 10x13cm and randomly stamp using the VersaMark pad. Rub Pearl Ex over the stamped images. Mount this onto a piece of navy card so that you have a small border all the way around.

4 Paint the Dragonfly with the Pearl Ex paints.

5 Assemble, using the example as a guide.

Butterfly Wishes
by Christi Snow

Materials:
- ☐ lilac, olive green, navy, blue and cream card
- ☐ Non Sequitor Stamps On Gossamer Wings from Blade Rubber
- ☐ Aloe Vera, Night Sky & Pretty Petunia VersaMagic chalk pads
- ☐ black inkpad
- ☐ clear embossing powder
- ☐ watercolour pencils
- ☐ waterbrush pen

To create:

1 On a 12x7.5cm piece of cream card, stamp two large butterflies in black ink. Colour these using the watercolour pencils and waterbrush pen.

2 Stamp the 'Butterfly Wishes' randomly across the background using second generation stamping. Sponge on additional inks until you're happy with the way that it looks. Apply the shattered glass technique (pages 68–69) and mount this onto a piece of 12.5x8cm navy card.

3 Mount a piece of 12.5x17.5cm olive green card onto the base card.

4 Use a scrap of blue card and a scrap of lilac card that measure 5cm wide and mount these onto a piece of navy card, with a small border all the way around.

5 Assemble using the example as a guide.

Refer back to pages 68–69 for a step-by-step to the cracked glass technique featured in the cards on this page

Tools for the job

✿ shrink plastic
✿ heat tool
✿ chalks or inks to decorate

Shrinky Dinks

Plenty of fun can be had creating perfect customised embellishments for your cards using shrink plastic. We show you how...

Everyone loves to use embellishments on their cards, but you can't always find exactly what you want. The answer is to make your own using shrink plastic. This fantastic product has a multitude of uses. It generally comes in A4 sheets and is available in four colours – white, black, clear and milky. As expected, each colour gives a totally different result. You can alter the colour yourself by using a variety of mediums, including permanent markers, inks, heat-set inks, pencil crayons and chalks.

There are many ways to create your design. You could draw your own image with a permanent marker and cut it out, or use a punch or rubber stamp to create a shape. The plastic image will be very thin, but when heated it will shrink to approx 45% of its size and be about 1/16" thick. If you're colouring your image, it's best to do it before shrinking, but be warned the colours you apply will intensify with heat, eg light pink will become dark pink.

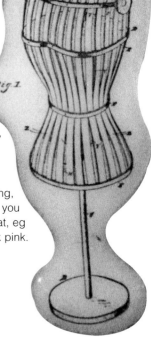

step 1 *On a heat-proof surface, heat the pre-cut shrink plastic using a heat gun. If you want holes in the finished piece, make sure to punch them before you start heating.*

step 2 *Warning: the plastic will start to curl, twist and bend. Don't panic – this is supposed to happen. Keep heating until it uncurls and lies flat.*

step 3 *When the plastic curls, it can occasionally stick to itself – if this happens, you'll need to pull the offending pieces carefully apart. The plastic will be very hot, so take care not to burn yourself.*

ⓘ **Shrinky dinks are shapes made from paper-thin plastic that has been stamped or punched, cut, then baked in an oven. The heat shrinks the plastic to form items suitable for jewellery, embellishments and trinkets**

Plastics

Play
by Christi Snow

Materials:
- ☐ Stamps Happen, Inc. Floating Softly stamp
- ☐ Derwent watercolour pencils
- ☐ Lucky Squirrel Polyshrink white shrink plastic
- ☐ Gin-X Desperately Seeking Summer patterned paper
- ☐ white floral brads
- ☐ green gingham ribbon
- ☐ black inkpad

To create:
1. Stamp the image onto white shrink plastic and colour it.
2. Punch two holes on the upper corners of the image and shrink. Tie a ribbon to the top of the shrink plastic and attach it to the card using a brad.
3. Finish the card with two strips of co-ordinating patterned papers and brads on the lower-left corner of the card.

Dress Form
by Trish Latimer

Materials:
- ☐ white, pink & black cardstocks
- ☐ pink & back gingham ribbon
- ☐ vellum
- ☐ hooks & eyes
- ☐ shrink plastic
- ☐ pink brad
- ☐ Stampington Dress Form, Buttons & Lace and Frayed Fabric stamps
- ☐ black pigment ink

To create:
1. Stamp the frayed fabric twice onto pink cardstock, and attach sets of hooks and eyes. Matt onto black cardstock. Stamp the buttons and lace onto pink cardstock and matt onto black cardstock.
2. Stamp the dress form twice, once onto torn-edged vellum, and once onto shrink plastic. Shrink the plastic with a heat gun, and edge with pink ink. Attach the vellum to the buttons and lace stamped panel using a brad.
3. Secure the shrink plastic dress form to the vellum. Tie the ribbon around the card blank, and attach the two prepared panels.

Shrink plastic will buckle and curl as it shrinks. Don't panic: this is normal. As it cools and finishes shrinking, it will flatten out again

With Love
by Stephanie Freame

Materials:
- [ ] Denami rubberstamp
- [ ] Marvy Le Plume pens
- [ ] Ranger Big & Bossy inkpad
- [ ] clear embossing powder
- [ ] white peel-off letters
- [ ] clear shrink plastic
- [ ] StäzOn black inkpad
- [ ] watercolour paper
- [ ] Ranger Glossy Accents
- [ ] blue & white cardstocks
- [ ] ribbons
- [ ] 3D foam pads

To create:

1 Stamp and clear-emboss the flower onto the white cardstock. Colour the background using a waterbrush and the Marvy pens.

2 Stamp the flower onto the watercolour paper using StäzOn ink. Colour with Marvy pens, trim, then mount it onto the blue cardstock and mount again. Finish both the flowers with the Glossy Accents.

3 Stamp three flowers onto shrink plastic, trim and heat. Assemble all the other embellishments and create the card design.

Thanks
by Lousette Ashton

Materials:
- [ ] white DL card blank
- [ ] Bazzill Chatterbox Dark Olive cardstock
- [ ] white shrink plastic
- [ ] Junkitz Ringz jump ring
- [ ] Making Memories Heidi large alphabet rub-ons

To create:

1 Use the flower template to draw a freehand daisy onto white shrink plastic, colour the inside with yellow pencil and outline with black permanent marker. Shrink as per the manufacturer's instructions.

2 Glue a wide strip of torn olive-coloured cardstock onto the top third of a DL-sized card blank, and use a compass cutter to cut a circular aperture in the centre. Cut another circle just smaller than the aperture and mount the daisy onto this using 3D pads.

3 Hang the daisy circle in the aperture using a jump ring, and finish off with rub-on lettering and three punched holes on either side of the aperture.

Plastics

New Home
by Dyan Reaveley

Materials:
- [ ] black & white card
- [ ] white shrink plastic
- [ ] permanent black marker
- [ ] foam squares

To create:
1. Take a piece of white card and score and fold it in half to make a tall A5 card. Place this to one side.
2. Trace the two images onto white shrink plastic using a black permanent marker. Cut them out, leaving a narrow border of white. Shrink both pieces and flatten.
3. Cut a strip of black card and attach it to the white card. Place foam pads on the back of each item and position on the card.

Exam Congratulations
by Dyan Reaveley

Materials:
- [ ] white card
- [ ] red card
- [ ] A Stamp In The Hand background text N-1772
- [ ] white shrink plastic
- [ ] black shrink plastic
- [ ] black StäzOn ink
- [ ] black tassel
- [ ] red ribbon
- [ ] black eyelets
- [ ] foam squares

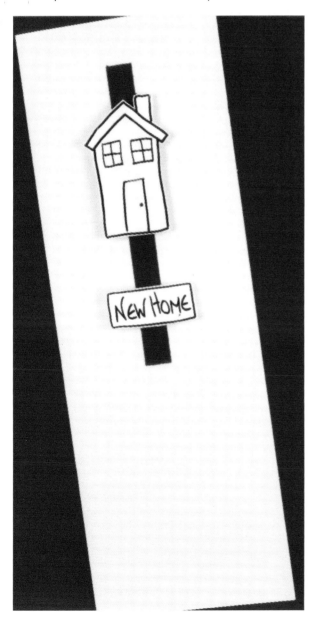

To create:
1. Cut and score a card, then fold it in half to form your base card. Put this to one side.
2. Cut a square out of black shrink plastic and punch a hole in the middle. Shrink and flatten. Attach the tassel through the hole.
3. Cut a square of white shrink plastic. Ink up the writing stamp with black StäzOn and stamp the plastic all over. Shrink, and whilst hot, roll up into a scroll shape. Leave to cool. Then tie a piece of red ribbon around it.
4. Take a square of white card and edge with black StäzOn ink. Stamp writing diagonally and attach to a red square using black eyelets. Edge with black ink.
5. Take the folded base card and stamp writing across it diagonally. Attach the red and white card to it centrally.
6. Attach foam squares to the scroll and mortar board, then fix them to the centre of card.

Tools for the job

✿ shrink plastic
✿ heat tool
✿ chalks or inks to
   decorate
✿ stamps

Intaglio

Although this stamping technique produces complicated-looking end results, it's surprisingly easy to do

Intaglio (in-tal-eo) is an Italian term that translates as 'a design produced in relief'. In real terms, this means pressing something into a receptive surface, in order to make an imprint. The technique can be used to create designs in clay, Friendly Plastic or UTEE – but, in this instance, we're creating with shrink plastic. Anything with a good texture can be used to imprint into shrink plastic, but all the projects here were created using rubberstamps. The stamps need to be deeply etched and have bold lines – detailed pictures with fine lines don't tend to work as well.

Shrink plastic is manufactured by heating a sheet of plastic and stretching it in two directions, then allowing it to cool. When the plastic is reheated, it reverts to its original size: about 45% of its stretched size and 2mm thick. Shrink plastic is available in four basic types: clear, which is good for a glass-like finish; translucent, for a softer look; white, for a crisp clean finish that shows colours and details well; and black, which gives a very dramatic look to any project. Shrink plastic can be heated using a heat gun (as we do in this project) or on a baking sheet in a hot oven.

step 1 *Shrink the plastic as shown on page 72.*

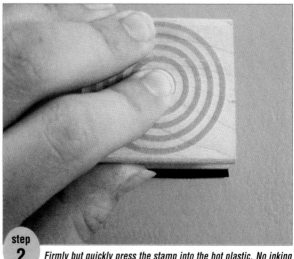

step 2 *Firmly but quickly press the stamp into the hot plastic. No inking is required, though inking the stamp with a heat-set ink will add colour to the impression.*

ℹ️ **Intaglio (pronounced in-TAHL-yo) is an Italian word for indentation; to cut or incise. In this instance the image is impressed into shrink plastic, although the technique is used with wood, metals and gems**

Green Spirals
by Trish Latimer

Materials:
- ☐ green cardstock
- ☐ gold cardstock
- ☐ 3 squares of mat board
- ☐ gold thread & eyelets
- ☐ clear embossing inkpad
- ☐ UTEE
- ☐ 3 shades of green embossing powder
- ☐ heat gun
- ☐ spiral stamp

To create:

1 Cover each square of mat board with embossing ink and sprinkle with UTEE. Repeat. For the third layer, use a normal green embossing powder. Whilst the powder is still hot, press a spiral stamp into it.

2 Adhere the three squares to a gold then green mat. Adhere a torn-edge panel to a green card blank and add eyelets.

3 Weave gold thread through the eyelets. Adhere the panel containing the three squares to the card blank.

Shrink plastic will buckle and curl as it shrinks. Don't panic – this is normal. As it cools and finishes shrinking, it will flatten out again

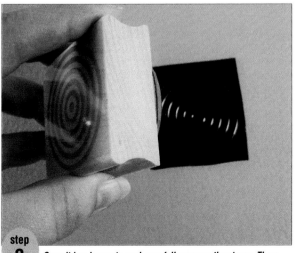

step 3 *Once it has begun to cool, carefully remove the stamp. There will be a debossed impression left in the plastic. Leave the plastic for about 15 minutes to enable it to set and cool.*

step 4 *Use metallic rub-ons, Krylon pen or heat-set ink to highlight your design. If you decide on the ink, you'll need to give it a quick blast with the heat gun in order for it to set.*

Plastics

Love
by Sue Roddis

Materials:
- [ ] black & pale pink cardstocks
- [ ] black shrink plastic
- [ ] metallic rub-ons
- [ ] clear embossing powder
- [ ] gold embossing powder
- [ ] black pigment inkpad
- [ ] VersaMark inkpad
- [ ] gold marker pen
- [ ] Hero Arts Old French Writing text stamp
- [ ] Magenta Love stamp

To create:

1 Cut three heart shapes from pre-sanded shrink plastic. Heat to shrink, and continue to heat for a few seconds after the shrinking process is complete, to ensure that the plastic is soft. Press the stamp into the plastic, holding in place until it has cooled.

2 Colour the hearts with metallic rub-ons in different colours, dip into clear embossing powder and heat. Stamp and emboss the pink cardstock with the script stamp and gold embossing powder, adding extra embossing ink and powder to the edges.

3 Score and fold the black card, then adhere the gold embossed piece and the three hearts. Draw two lines with the gold marker to finish.

A Bouquet of Roses
by Trish Latimer

Materials:
- [ ] white C6 card blank
- [ ] Bazzill Basics Romance Pink cardstock
- [ ] silver card for matting
- [ ] translucent shrink plastic
- [ ] fibres
- [ ] silver embossing powder
- [ ] Brilliance Pearlescent Orchid ink
- [ ] clear embossing pad
- [ ] Hero Arts Delicate Rose Stems stamp
- [ ] silver Krylon pen

To create:

1 Take a piece of shrink plastic and colour it using the direct-to-paper technique with the Brilliance Pearlescent Orchid ink.

2 Punch two holes in the shrink plastic, then heat it with a heat gun until the plastic has uncurled and lies flat.

3 Press the stamp firmly into the hot plastic and remove. When it has cooled, highlight and edge the piece by dabbing on Krylon with a finger. Using the dauber, gently sponge around the edges with Brilliance Pearlescent Orchid, then set the ink with a heat gun.

4 Using smaller pieces of shrink plastic, stamp the roses with the Brilliance ink. Shrink the plastic using the heat gun. Once it has cooled, sponge the edges with Brilliance ink and heat-set.

5 On the top-right corner of the card blank, stamp the roses using clear embossing ink and sprinkle silver embossing powder over the image. Heat until the embossing powder has melted. Once cool, roughly colour with pink chalks.

6 Add a torn-edged pink panel to the card blank. Tie the large piece of shrink plastic to the centre with flowers.

7 Matt the smaller piece of shrink plastic onto silver and pink card, then adhere it to the bottom-right corner of the blank.

Intaglio Jewellery Set

by Trish Latimer

Materials:

- ☐ translucent shrink plastic
- ☐ Sizzix Circle 2 die
- ☐ silver Krylon pen
- ☐ silver earring findings
- ☐ silver eyepins
- ☐ selection of purple beads
- ☐ round-nosed jewellery pliers
- ☐ silver chain
- ☐ silver jump rings
- ☐ Brilliance Platinum Planet ink, Pearlescent Purple ink, Victorian Violet ink
- ☐ Penny Black Love Maze stamp

To create:

1. Cut three circles of translucent shrink plastic using the Sizzix die cutter and punch four holes into each one. Then cut three random shapes from shrink plastic, punching a hole in the top of each.

2. Using all three colours of ink, sponge randomly over the six pieces of shrink plastic.

3. Taking each piece in turn, heat it until it is shrunken and flat, then impress the stamp into the hot plastic.

4. Once all six have shrunk and cooled, rub Krylon pen over them to highlight the debossed areas. Then edge the pieces with Krylon.

5. Now you're ready to assemble the jewellery. Attach a randomly shaped piece of shrink plastic to the central hole in one of the circular pieces of shrink plastic. Using an eyepin, thread on some purple beads. Attach one end of the eyepin to the circular piece, and the other end to the randomly shaped piece. Do this three times, so each circular piece of shrink plastic has a beaded drop hanging from the central hole.

6. On either side of this central drop is another beaded drop, this time with no shrink plastic. Again using eyepins, thread on some purple beads, and attach to the holes either side of the beaded shrink plastic drop. Do this six times, so all the circles have beaded drops.

7. Thread a jump ring through the top hole on all three circles of shrink plastic, and thread a couple of purple seed beads onto them.

8. Attach silver ear wires onto two of the circles, threading them through the jump rings.

9. Affix a silver chain to the remaining circle, threading it through the jump ring.

Verdigris Box

by Trish Latimer

Materials:

- ☐ papier mâché box blank
- ☐ Lumiere Emerald & Gold acrylic paint
- ☐ faux keyhole brad
- ☐ key charm
- ☐ fibres
- ☐ translucent shrink plastic
- ☐ gold Krylon pen
- ☐ Brilliance Pearlescent Emerald & Galaxy Gold ink
- ☐ Penny Black Love Maze stamp

To create:

1. Paint the box and its lid with Emerald acrylic paint, then stipple gold acrylic paint into it whilst wet. To achieve the textured effect, heat the wet paint with the heat gun. It will boil and bubble, then leave you with a lumpy, weathered look. Do this in a well-ventilated place as the fumes are strong.

2. Add the faux keyhole brad by pushing the prongs through the box and securing them. Tie co-ordinating fibres around the box, then add a key charm.

3. Take six pieces of shrink plastic, each measuring 8x7cm, and sponge them all randomly with the two Brilliance inks.

4. Heat each piece of shrink plastic in turn until it's shrunken and flat, then impress the stamp into the hot plastic.

5. Once you've done all six, rub Krylon pen over them to highlight (using your finger is the easiest way). Edge each piece with Krylon.

6. Adhere the pieces of shrink plastic to the lid of the box.

Plastics

Tools for the job

✿ resist stamp pad
✿ inky roller brayer
✿ stamps
✿ dye-based inks

Resist inks

The magical resist technique creates stunning customised backgrounds and ghost effects in your stamping. Easy to achieve, all you need to do is make sure you use the right inks

Resist stamping is a simple technique that can be done by just about any stamper at any skill level. It uses tools that most crafters already have in their cabinets and complements any style. Resist stamping can be applied to create background papers with gorgeous tone-on-tone effects, or it can be used for focal images in embellishments or even for the centrepiece of a card. The effects created by resist stamping vary depending on the inks and stamps used. From elegant and fancy to fun and funky, you'll create some fabulous papers using this technique.

Once you've mastered the basics, start experimenting. The effects that can be created using resist stamping are almost limitless. Different colours can be layered on top of the resist, blending together to create some beautiful effects. It's also possible to apply several layers of the resist, creating different colours within the stamped images. The resist can be used as a shadow by stamping normal stamped images on top of and slightly off centre from the resist images.

ℹ Resist ink creates a resistant effect on the second ink that is applied. This is most dramatic when the colour underneath is lighter and brighter than the colour(s) on top. The colours laid down first appear to pop out from the surface. This technique works best on gloss paper

step 1 *One of the basic tools needed for resist stamping is an inkpad to create the resist. This can be a VersaMark pad, an embossing pad or a resist pad. Also needed are stamps, coloured inkpads, a brayer, and white cardstock. Using the VersaMark pad or resist stamp pad, ink up your chosen stamp.*

step 2 *Stamp your image all over your background paper. A prepared work surface is a must. Be sure to have a large piece of paper to work on because the brayered ink will be going over the edges of the project. It's also important for the surface to be free of any dust or particles, as these create an uneven brayered effect.*

Floral Elegance
by Christi Snow

Materials:
- ☐ Anna Griffin Roses patterned paper
- ☐ All Night Media Anna Griffin stamps
- ☐ 7gypsies metal ribbon buckle
- ☐ VersaMark inkpad
- ☐ white glossy, cream, sky blue & dark brown cardstock
- ☐ pink inkpad
- ☐ brayer
- ☐ ribbon
- ☐ brown chalk

To create:

1 Stamp the images onto the white glossy card using clear VersaMark to create the resist. Trim and mount onto the sky blue card.

2 Assemble the card, chalking around the edge of the cream cardstock with the brown chalk.

3 Finish the card with the buckle and ribbon.

step 3 *Apply the colour, using (and frequently re-inking) a brayer. Be warned: when you start doing this, it's going to look awful and you're going to hate it, but keep at it!*

step 4 *The effect works better if the brayering is done in only one direction. Eventually, it all evens out. Don't be put off by the colours being so uneven throughout the majority of the brayering. This is because you haven't brayered on enough colour yet.*

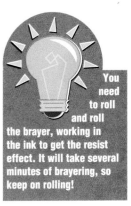

You need to roll and roll the brayer, working in the ink to get the resist effect. It will take several minutes of brayering, so keep on rolling!

Poetry
by Sue Roddis

Materials:
- [ ] cream & brown card
- [ ] Perfect Medium clear embossing inkpad
- [ ] clear embossing powder
- [ ] walnut ink
- [ ] Memories brown inkpad
- [ ] sheer ribbon
- [ ] spiral clip
- [ ] K&Co Life's Journey Clocks & Lures 2 embellishment
- [ ] Penny Black Irises stamp
- [ ] Catslife Press Poetry stamp
- [ ] Hero Arts Text stamp

To create:

1 Cut a piece of card to fit the front of a folded A5 card.

2 Ink the Irises stamp with the Perfect Medium inkpad and stamp it into the centre of the card. Add clear embossing powder and heat to melt the powder.

3 Paint across the whole card with walnut ink. Leave it to dry. Wipe any excess off the embossed image.

4 Once dry, stamp the text image lightly across the whole card, again wiping any ink off the embossed image.

5 Stamp the word 'POETRY' in the top right-hand corner using the brown Memories inkpad.

6 Add the ribbon, spiral clip and watch embellishment to the left side of the card.

7 Colour the edges of a folded A5 brown card with the brown Memories inkpad then attach the other card to it.

Everlasting Blues
by Trish Latimer

Materials:
- [ ] blue cardstock
- [ ] white glossy cardstock
- [ ] VersaMark inkpad
- [ ] large eyelets
- [ ] blue ribbon
- [ ] shades of blue ink
- [ ] silver Krylon pen
- [ ] word and collage stamps

To create:

1 Stamp the collage stamp with VersaMark on a glossy cardstock panel, and heat to set the ink. Sponge shades of blue ink over the whole panel.

2 Over-stamp the collage again with a dark blue ink, and also stamp words. Fix three large eyelets to the panel, and thread blue ribbon through them.

3 Matt the panel onto torn-edged cardstock, and matt this onto a dark blue card blank. Splatter silver Krylon pen ink on the bottom corner.

Cherish Yesterday
by Sue Roddis

Materials:
- ☐ white, pale & darker blue card
- ☐ Perfect Medium clear embossing inkpad
- ☐ Vivid Rainbow Desert Sky dye inkpad
- ☐ brayer
- ☐ Stampington Parisian Shell stamp
- ☐ Hero Arts Cherish Yesterday stamp
- ☐ Clear Choice Leaf Decor stamp

To create:

1 Ink the Parisian Shell stamp with the Perfect Medium inkpad and stamp onto a piece of white card. Leave to dry for a while or heat gently with a heat tool.

2 Ink the brayer from the Vivid inkpad then roll it across the stamped image. Depending upon the intensity of the colour, re-ink the brayer and roll it again, making sure to align the colours. Rub gently over the image with a paper towel to remove any excess ink.

3 Trim around the image and mount it onto a slightly bigger piece of dark blue card.

4 Use the Perfect Medium inkpad to stamp the quote onto white card. Colour it in the same way as the main image, trim around it and mount it onto a piece of darker blue card.

5 Fold a light blue A5 card in half. Use the Leaf Decor stamp and the Vivid inkpad to stamp around the edges of the card.

6 Mount the shell image to the centre of the card and add the quote underneath.

Tools for the job

✿ clear embossing inkpad
✿ clear embossing powder
✿ stamp
✿ metal sheets
✿ acrylic paint

Batik on metal

Traditionally used as a way to dye and decorate fabrics, the batik method can also be applied to metal to create a wonderful resist effect, with a little help from our old friend UTEE

In many ways, resisting with Ultra Thick Embossing Enamel (UTEE) is similar to the ancient craft of batik as applied to handmade papers and fabrics. But creating the resist pattern on the very different medium of metal requires a special combination of resist and batik techniques.

Embossing ink and powder are added to the metal sheet or embellishment, which is then either painted of inked (using a solvent alcohol ink). When the metal is ironed between sheets of paper towels, the embossing powders melt off into the sheets – leaving behind a resist effect on the treated metal. This same technique can be used on a variety of different surfaces and materials.

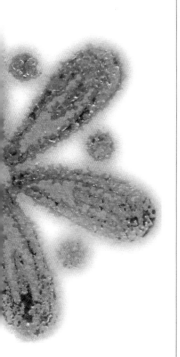

i Batik is an Indonesian technique traditionally used on fabrics where a wax- or oil-type treatment is applied to the paper or fabric prior to the colour or dye. The oil or wax is removed by melting it, leaving a resist effect in the material. The technique can be adapted for use on metals with the help of UTEE

Summer Flower
by Natalie O'Shea

Materials:
☐ blue & yellow cardstock
☐ Junkitz Summer Collentionz patterned papers
☐ blue & yellow chalk inkpads
☐ Making Memories metal plaque, metal words, foam stamp & brads
☐ blue & yellow acrylic paint
☐ fabric & paper flowers
☐ Lasting Impressions Sentimetal greeting
☐ blue & yellow acrylic paints
☐ various metal washers from B&Q
☐ ArtEmboss pewter – medium-weight metal sheet
☐ UTEE
☐ Mod Podge gloss glaze

To create:

1 Make a base card from blue striped card, round the top-right and bottom-right corners, and edge with yellow chalk ink.

2 Cut a rectangle of yellow patterned paper, round the corners and place vertically down the left-hand side of the base card.

3 Cut a square of blue patterned paper, round the corners and attach towards the right-hand side of the base card.

4 Create a rectangle of patterned metal sheet using the technique described on the facing page and stick it to the top half of the base card.

5 Attach some fabric flowers with a button centre to the bottom-right corner of the base card.

6 Add a metal greeting to the left of the flower using 3D foam pads.

step 1 Cut your metal sheet to size. Rub an anti-static bag across the top to remove any finger marks or residue. Using a VersaMark pad, ink your stamp and stamp the image randomly several times over the metal sheet.

step 2 Making sure the ink doesn't dry, gently sprinkle the image with Ultra Thick Embossing Enamel (UTEE). Shake off the excess and return to the jar. Use a soft brush to remove any UTEE that has stuck where it shouldn't have.

step 3 Using your heat tool, warm the embossing powder in sweeping actions to ensure that you don't overheat one area. Once at the right temperature, you'll see the UTEE start to melt. Continue until you have a level embossed image. Allow it to cool.

step 4 Using a cotton wool ball, gently dab some blue paint over a couple of areas of the metal sheet. Ensure that you don't have any harsh edges by applying lighter pressure at the edges.

step 5 The blue paint will dry quickly. When you can see the edges drying, gently apply the yellow paint in the gaps between the blue. Make sure the colours blend together and don't look like completely different sections.

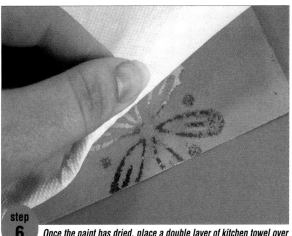

step 6 Once the paint has dried, place a double layer of kitchen towel over the metal sheet. Using a dry iron, gently iron over the sheet. You will need to do this several times – you'll see when the UTEE starts to melt again, as it will leave a mark on the kitchen towel. Remove the towel to remove most of the UTEE, leaving the metal showing through.

Tools for the job

✿ peel-offs
✿ ink or chalks
✿ cardstock

Resist with peel-offs

Using a peel-off or sticker as the resist element enables you to create quick and simple, yet effective, backgrounds

Rather than a peel-off being the finishing touch to your greetings card, here it is being used as a tool to create backgrounds. The best type of peel-offs to use for this are images with open designs, so that the material you are using for resist will show through.

This technique is similar to all the others in as much as you apply the design that will become the resist, in this instance the peel-off, then you apply the ink, chalks or embossing powder. Once set and dry, you can peel away the designs and the pattern will show through as the original colour of the paper.

Materials:
☐ white card
☐ black present peel-off - Françoise Collection
☐ Rocket Red brilliance inkpad
☐ stipple brush
☐ Happy Christmas peel-off

To create:

1 Cut white card to A5 and fold. Take two present peel-offs and place near the top of the card.

2 Stipple using the red ink over the peel-offs. . Remove peeloffs and position further down the card. Stipple with red ink.

3 Repeat until the card is covered and attach Happy Christmas greeting.

Happy Christmas
by Dyan Reaveley

ℹ️ **Resist ink creates a resistant effect** on the second ink that is applied. This is most dramatic when the colour underneath is lighter and brighter than the colour(s) on top. The colours laid down first appear to pop out from the surface. This technique works best on gloss paper

step 1 *Position your peel-off images onto your card blank or background paper. If you only have a few, that is fine, as you can reposition them as you go along.*

step 2 *Using an inkpad, apply the ink directly to the paper. Alternatively, you could use a piece of craft foam to achieve this look, along with chalks or embossing powders.*

Thank You
by Tracey Kirkby

Materials:
- ☐ white cardstock
- ☐ silver cardstock
- ☐ Anita's Outline stickers
- ☐ Whispers Thank You stamp
- ☐ Black Sparkle embossing powder
- ☐ VersaMark inkpad
- ☐ silver pen

To create:

1 Stick the peel-off onto cardstock then cover with embossing ink and embossing powder. Once cool, peel away the stickers.

2 Using the silver pen, colour in the impression in the embossed area.

3 Mount these squares onto silver cardstock then arrange the elements on the white card blank.

step 3 *Move the stickers as you go along to create the random patterns. This way you do not need to buy sheets with the same design – just three or four will suffice.*

Tools for the job

✿ lacé template
✿ craft knife
✿ cardstock & patterned papers
✿ cutting mat
✿ low-tack tape
✿ bone folder
✿ stylus
✿ ruler

Folding

Lacé

An intricate method of folding that originated in Holland, this is by no means an easy technique, but it is easy!

Lacé is known by many other names, including the incire technique or lassay. There isn't too much to tell about the procedure, as it's simply the technique of cutting through paper with a craft knife and using a metal template as a cutting guide. The triangles or cut shapes are then folded over outwards and pushed back through the slits. This can take a little time to perfect. You'll need to work out the best way to hold the knife and which papers to use, though it quickly becomes apparent just how

versatile the technique can be. So be patient!

Lacé can be applied to handmade cards, bookmarks, and almost any other papercraft. Most cardstocks and papers are suitable, but the best effect is achieved by using a duo-coloured, double-sided cardstock, which shows a complementary colour when folded. If you don't have double-sided cardstock, you could ink, chalk or otherwise colour the reverse of your paper where the design will be cut from.

Congratulations
by Natalie O'Shea

Materials
☐ purple pearlescent card
☐ plain purple card
☐ purple embroidered paper
☐ baby vellum
☐ lacé template 8
☐ craft knife
☐ peel-off greeting

To create:

1. Attach your template to the centre of a square of vellum, and cut where indicated on the template. Remove the template, then fold each triangle back and tuck it under the previous one.

2. Attach the vellum square onto a square of pearlescent purple card, then onto embroidered purple card, and finally onto a base card made from plain purple card.

3. Attach the peel-off greeting to the centre of the card.

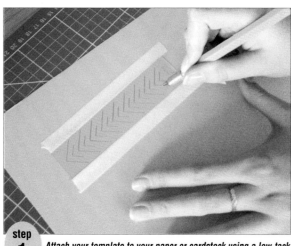

step 1 *Attach your template to your paper or cardstock using a low-tack repositionable tape. Then, holding your knife at a 90° angle, cut into the centre of the design on the template.*

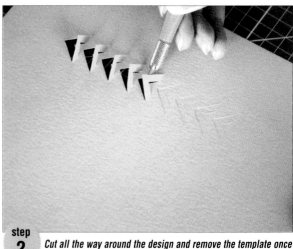

step 2 *Cut all the way around the design and remove the template once you've finished. Score the fold lines of the design.*

Cherish by Sue Roddis

Materials
- ☐ A5 cream card
- ☐ cream handmade paper
- ☐ gold cardstock
- ☐ gold tassel
- ☐ Paperbag Studios Vintage Collage sheet
- ☐ lacé template 2
- ☐ Artwords Cherish stamp
- ☐ Ranger black inkpad

To create:

1 Use your lacé template and knife to cut just part of the design in the handmade paper, as shown. Fold back the cut sections. Cut a slot at the bottom of the design to tuck in the last triangle, and attach the tassel here.

2 Cut the photo from the collage sheet, mount it onto the gold cardstock and attach it to the right-hand side of the handmade paper.

3 Stamp Cherish onto a piece of gold paper and adhere this below the photo. Place a piece of gold card behind the lacé design. Adhere the handmade paper to the cream card.

step 3 *Lift the triangles from the design and fold them back neatly with a bone folder. Tuck the points under the flaps on the design.*

Happy Birthday by Kirsty Wiseman

Materials
- ☐ cream ribbed card blank
- ☐ pink cardstock
- ☐ patterned paper
- ☐ gem flowers
- ☐ wire
- ☐ ribbon
- ☐ Hero Arts letter stamps
- ☐ Ranger pink inkpad

To create:

1 Cut the lacé design from the pink cardstock. Cut around the design to form the shape of a flower.

2 Attach a piece of torn paper to the base of the card. Tuck in a piece of shaped wire to make a stem, and affix with glue.

3 Adhere the lacé design to the card and embellish with gems. Finish off the card with ribbon, a stamped title and additional gem embellishments as shown.

ⓘ Lacé is a cutting and folding technique using a specialist metal template and sharp knife. It originated in Holland, though it has been adapted and modernised over the last few years. A design is cut in the direction of the arrows on the template using a sharp pointed knife as your tool. You then fold the triangles outwards, pushing them back through the slits

Folding

Tools for the job

✿ quilling tool
✿ quilling papers
✿ glue
✿ a pattern

Folding

Quilling

This fascinating but fiddly hobby is often the first papercraft people come across as children. But adult crafters would be wrong to dismiss it, as its unique technique produces some attractive results

The art of paper quilling dates back a couple of centuries to a time when nuns used the gold edges trimmed from Bible pages to create simple but beautiful works of artistry. The scraps of paper were wrapped around goose quills to create coiled shapes, which is where the name quilling came from.

It is an easy, inexpensive and enjoyable craft, suitable for all ages. A combination of tight winding, curling, creasing and gluing are used to form the designs, that can then be used to decorate greeting and gift tags. There are two basic shapes: coils and scrolls.

The most important thing to remember when quilling is that less is most definitely more – use as little glue as possible as this helps the design to look delicate. When you pinch the coil, pinch over the glued edge, which will hide the glue. Pinching and squeezing the finished coil between your fingers and thumbs is how you form your desired shapes.

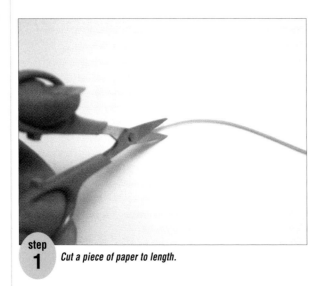

step 1 *Cut a piece of paper to length.*

step 2 *Slot the paper into the end of the tool and begin to twist, holding the coil tightly in your fingertips as it develops to keep the tension*

step 3 *Once the coil is complete, glue the end of the paper down.*

step 4 *Shape to suit your design.*

The Complete Cardmaking Handbook

Baby Boy Jennie Findlay

Materials
- ☐ various quilling papers
- ☐ white mulberry paper
- ☐ ribbons
- ☐ gold thread
- ☐ inkpad

To create:

1 Make four blue baby feet by coiling and shaping 3mm-wide paper. Ink the edge of the white mulberry paper with gold thread, and attach with double-sided tape.

2 Glue the feet onto the mulberry paper with PVA glue, and tie short lengths of patterned blue ribbon to the right-hand side of the aperture.

3 Glue rickrack along the left of the card. Ink the pop-out section retained from the centre of the aperture, and fix to the front with PVA glue.

Less is more and practice makes perfect – familiar sayings, but they sum up successful quilling

The shapes
Basic coil Not pinched or shaped
Teardrop Pinch at one end
Eye Pinch at both ends
Triangle Shape with fingers and thumbs
Square Shape by squeezing in with fingers and thumbs

Folding

Folding

Hanging Roses by Jennie Findlay

Materials
☐ various quilling papers
☐ jump ring
☐ card blank with an
   aperture

To create:

1 Make the roses by twisting and folding the paper as you turn the quilling tool.

2 Glue four lengths of 6mm-wide red paper together, and attach the 6mm roses onto the end of the strip.

3 Pierce a hole in the end of the rose strip and the top of the aperture. Attach the strip with a jump ring.

4 Glue the retained section that pops out from the aperture to the front of the card, and glue the three small roses to the end. Finally, glue a 3mm strip in a matching shade to that used for the roses to the left edge of the card.

Dragonfly by Jennie Findlay

Materials
☐ various quilling papers
☐ mulberry flowers
☐ silver embroidery thread
☐ aperture card blank

To create:

1 Make the dragonfly wings from pink and purple 3mm strips.

2 Glue the wings to a body of tightly rolled black 3mm strips, glued in a line.

3 Stick mulberry flowers in various shades and sizes to the bottom of the aperture, and adhere a section of deep blue mulberry paper in the aperture.

4 Suspend the dragonfly in the aperture, close to the flowers, using silver embroidery thread.

Targets by Jennie Findlay

Materials
- [ ] various quilling papers
- [ ] chalks
- [ ] card blank

To create:

1 Roll four target shapes of varying sizes from brown and pink 3mm paper.

2 Shade the background of the aperture with two shades of brown chalk, and glue the targets onto this background.

3 Glue the smallest target to the end of the pop-out section retained from the aperture. Then glue a short strip of 3mm pink to the length of the section.

4 Glue a strip of 3mm brown to the left edge of the front of the card to complete.

Sunflower by Jennie Findlay

Materials
- [ ] various quilling papers
- [ ] card blank

To create:

1 Make the sunflower head by rolling loose yellow rolls from 3mm paper and pinching into teardrop shapes, before attaching to a tight, brown roll of 3mm paper.

2 Glue to the background of the card using PVA. Glue together two strips of 3mm green and attach to the card below the sunflower head.

3 Fringe 6mm strips in co-ordinating shades of green, before gluing to the bottom of the card. To finish, pop out the end of the section from the aperture.

i Quilling is the art of creating decorative designs from thin strips of curled paper. Using simple tools, long strips of paper are tightly wound and released to form complex shapes. Also called paper filigree, the art has been practised since the Renaissance.

Tools for the job

- ✿ aperture card blank
- ✿ lightweight patterned papers
- ✿ a paper trimmer
- ✿ metal-edged ruler
- ✿ scissors
- ✿ pencil
- ✿ clear tape
- ✿ a pattern

Iris Folding

Sunset
by Trish Latimer

Materials

- ☐ shades of red/orange/ yellow papers
- ☐ black paper
- ☐ black cardstock
- ☐ red cardstock
- ☐ fibre
- ☐ palm tree stamp

To create:

1 Draw a rectangle on a sheet of paper and, using a ruler, draw lines across to represent where the paper will be laid down. This technique is called 'abstract iris folding' as it involves the same paper-layering techniques of regular iris folding, but the pattern doesn't lead the eye towards a central point.

2 Place the template under an aperture in black cardstock and, using folded paper strips, lay them over the template lines. Secure with sticky tape. Try to match the colours to those of a sunset.

3 When all the spaces on the template have been filled, turn over your work and adhere to a red card bank. Add a stamped and cutout palm tree, then fibres to finish.

This technique uses layers of folded strips of patterned papers, which combine to create unique spiral patterns. The name comes from the centre of the finished design typically resembling the iris of an eye

This simple way of paper folding is very popular, and you'll find numerous patterns available in books, magazines and online. The technique takes minimal practice to conquer, and once you have a go you will never look back! The results, however, looks anything but simple – you can create truly impressive effects, and when mixed with an aperture card, make great gifts and decorations.

Iris folding appeals to both experienced and new crafters, as it doesn't require many specialist materials or tools. You can advance from the easier patterns to the more sophisticated and complex, and in no time at all you will be an iris addict.

step 1 *Tape a copy of the folding pattern (the one with all the lines, numbers and letters on it) to your work surface; then tape the cardstock face down onto the pattern. Choose your scrap papers and cut to ¾" width (the length doesn't matter, you will trim it down as you go along). Keep the different scrap papers separated into piles.*

Vintage
by Sue Roddis

Materials
- ☐ A4 cream card
- ☐ white card
- ☐ Design Originals Iris Folding papers
- ☐ gold paper
- ☐ Paperbag Studios Vintage Collage sheet
- ☐ Fibrescraps E-Z Walnut Tintz in Tea Stain & Rust
- ☐ alphabet stickers
- ☐ gold peel-off border strips

To create:

1 Cut a square of white card to measure 14cm square. Cut a 10cm aperture in the centre. Colour the card using the walnut Tintz and leave to dry.

2 Lay the strips over the placement template and, following the pattern, glue down the strips of paper. Replace the last row with gold paper to give the photo a gold frame. Attach the photo in the centre.

3 Use gold peel-off strips to frame the edge of the aperture and decorate the corners. Fold the A4 cream card in half, attach the iris-folded piece and trim away the excess.

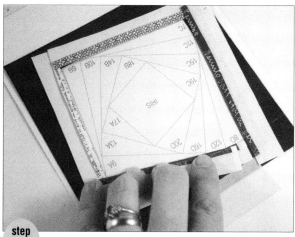

step 2 *Fold the edge of each strip over by a third. Take a folded strip of your first paper and place the edge directly on the pattern line (face down of course!). Follow the pattern around clockwise, alternating colours as you go: paper 1, paper 2, paper 3, paper 4, then back to paper 1, again overlapping as you go. Also remember to trim the edges as you go along, and to tape both the ends.*

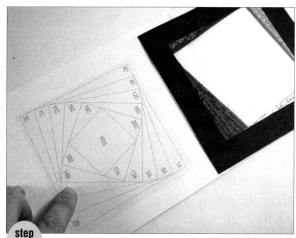

step 3 *By taping one side of the cardstock down you can lift it to check your work along the way. Fill the middle (or the iris) with a piece of shiny paper. Once you have completed the pattern, remove the cardstock from your work surfaces and carefully remove the tape from the edge. Cut the cardstock to centre your iris folding or to fit the front of your card.*

> ℹ️ **Iris folding is a technique that originated in Holland. Coloured strips of folded paper are taped into place over a pattern, creating a spiral design that resembles an iris. Originally papercrafters used strips from the patterned interior of envelopes, but now lightweight patterned and coloured papers are more commonly used**

Heart
by Sue Roddis

Materials
- ☐ A5 white card
- ☐ black card
- ☐ iris folding papers (from Iris Folding Papers book by Design Originals)
- ☐ masking tape
- ☐ heart punch
- ☐ Memories black inkpad
- ☐ Hero Arts Enjoy Life's Moments rubberstamp

To create:

1 Cut a piece of black card to measure 12x8cm. Cut a heart-shaped aperture in the card.

2 Choose three different iris folding papers, cut them into strips and fold over a small edge on each one.

3 Working in groups of the three papers, add them in a random fashion at the back of the aperture, using the technique shown below. The trick is to keep the papers evenly spaced and to have all three come to a point at one end. Start at one side of the heart and add the group of three papers, then go to the other side of the heart and add another group. Continue in this fashion, being intentionally random with the placements, until the whole of the aperture is filled.

4 Attach the black card to the top-left corner of a folded white A5 card.

5 Punch four hearts from a scrap of one of the folding papers, then attach these down the right-hand side of the black card.

6 Cut a strip of another of the papers to fit along the bottom of the card. Stamp the sentiment onto the strip of paper using the black inkpad. Attach the strip along the bottom of the card.

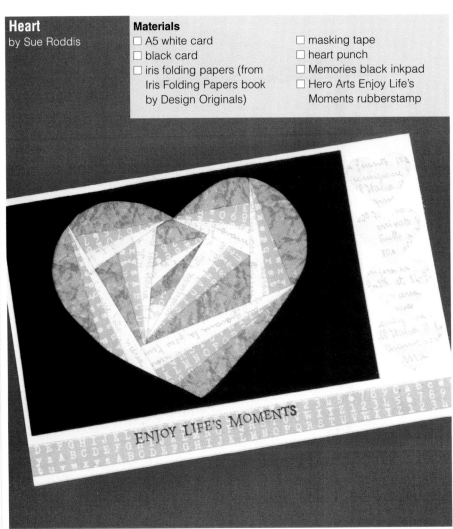

ENJOY LIFE'S MOMENTS

Freestyle Iris Folding

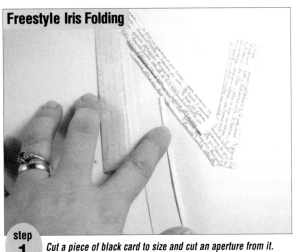

step 1
Cut a piece of black card to size and cut an aperture from it. This can be any size, as you are not working to a set pattern. Choose three different iris folding papers, cut them into strips and fold over a small edge on each one.

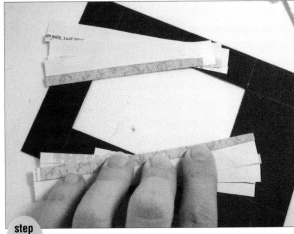

step 2
Working in groups of the three papers, add them in a random fashion at the back of the aperture. The trick is to keep the papers evenly spaced and to have all three come to a point at one end. Trim away the papers where they overlap the edges of the card.

Full iris folding instructions

1. Cut an aperture in your chosen piece of card, and choose the papers you are going to use. The number of different papers you need depends on the pattern you are working to. Cut the paper into strips. Again, the width of the strips and the number you need depends on the pattern. Generally you will need between four and eight strips of each paper.

2. Fold over the edge of each strip, so that the folded edge faces towards the centre of the pattern and gives a neat finish. Sort the strips into the different patterns, one set for each section of the pattern.

3. Place the aperture face down over the pattern and hold it in place with masking tape.

4. Fill each section of the pattern in turn, following the numbers so that the pattern spirals into the centre. Don't work one section and then the next, it won't work!

5. Stick the paper strips in place with small pieces of tape at the left and right sides of each strip. Alternatively use small amounts of PVA glue, making sure it doesn't seep through to the front.

6. Remove the card from the pattern. There will be a hole in the centre which can be filled with something appropriate to match the papers used.

7. The back of the work will need to be covered in some way to hide the strips of paper. You can do this by sticking the piece of card onto the front of a folded card, or by gluing another piece of card or paper over the back.

Materials
- ☐ A5 black card
- ☐ pink card
- ☐ iris folding papers (from *Iris Folding Papers* book by Design Originals)
- ☐ masking tape
- ☐ PVA glue or sticky tape
- ☐ Motivate Sentiments ROY510 & Ladies Accessories ROY580 rub-on sheets

Dream
by Sue Roddis

To create:

1 Cut a piece of pink card to measure 14x10cm. Cut an aperture measuring 8.5x7cm in the centre of the card.

2 Decide which of the folding papers you are going to use – you need two different ones, one for the corners and the second for the rest. Cut them into strips then into smaller pieces to fit the pattern. Fold over a thin edge on each piece.

3 Place the card with the aperture face down over the pattern and hold it in place with a strip of masking tape. Follow the pattern and attach the strips of folded paper, using either glue or sticky tape. When finished, remove the card from the pattern.

4 Apply the rub-on sentiments above and below the aperture.

5 For the centre of the aperture, apply the woman image onto a scrap of black card. Fasten this behind the aperture.

6 Attach the pink card to the front of a folded black card, making sure it is securely fastened around the edges.

■ Avoid using bulky card or embossed papers for the folded element. They can be difficult to handle and will bulk out your project
■ Save money by using scrap pieces of paper left over from other papercraft projects, or be resourceful and use party bags, gift-wrap, decorative envelopes or origami paper

Tools for the job

✿ a variety of seed beads
✿ beadling wire
✿ wire cutters
✿ beading mat

Beadlings

A piece of wire and a few beads can be brought to life as a beadling. These inexpensive embellishments will work perfectly with almost any theme and can be created in a matter of minutes

The beautiful craft of beading originated in Native American culture. The intricate peyote stitch was used for everything from jewellery to clothing. Originally the beads were carved from shells, coral, turquoise and other stones, copper and silver, wood, amber, ivory, and animal bones, horns, and teeth. Then, in the mid-1900s, glass beads were introduced by colonists who brought them from Europe – and have since become the most commonly used bead.

Beadlings are an adaptation of the traditional beading techniques, and the name reflects the fact that most of them simulate living objects. Usually the creatures are created with seed beads, although more intricate designs will incorporate other beads such as bugle beads.

By following this simple step-by-step, you'll master the basic stitch that the beadling is made from. Then you'll soon be able to easily construct exceptional shapes and creatures.

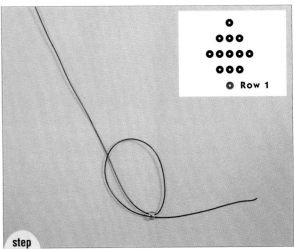

step 1 *Row 1: String one seed bead onto the centre of your wire. Bring the right-hand wire over the bead and thread it back through in the opposite direction, so that the two ends are pointing in different directions. As you pull the ends of the wire to tighten the wire loop around the bead, try to ensure that the bead stays in the middle so you have equal lengths on either side.*

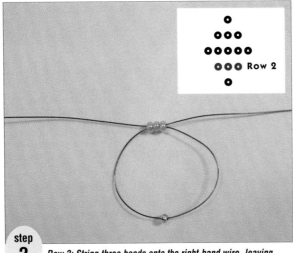

step 2 *Row 2: String three beads onto the right-hand wire, leaving them near the end. Take the left-hand wire and thread it back through the three beads in the opposite direction to the right-hand wire. Pull both wires carefully to tighten the loops around the bead – they should sit neatly above the bead you've already threaded.*

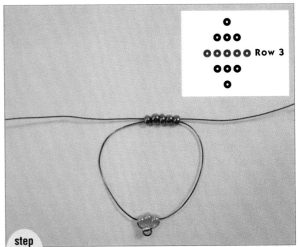

step 3 *Row 3: String five beads onto the right-hand wire and leave them near the end. Take the left-hand wire and thread it back through the beads, as above. Pull the wires tight.*

Angel by Lousette Ashton

Materials:
- □ various seed & bugle beads
- □ Making Memories eyelets
- □ ribbon
- □ card blank
- □ patterned paper
- □ black Zig Writer pen

To create:

1 Use the pattern at the back of the book and follow the technique shown to create the angel.

2 Cut the patterned paper to shape and adhere it to the card blank. Set two eyelets in the front of the card.

3 Attach the angel to the card using the ribbon threaded through the eyelets.

4 Write your message on the card.

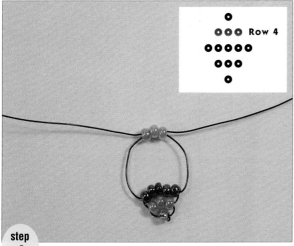

step 4 Row 4: String three beads onto the right-hand wire. Take the left-hand wire and thread it back through in the opposite direction. Pull the wires tight.

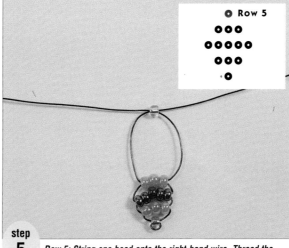

step 5 Row 5: String one bead onto the right-hand wire. Thread the left-hand wire back through in the opposite direction. Pull the wires tight. Either wrap the wires around the wire at the end of the row, or thread them through the last seed bead again to secure.

ⓘ Beadlings are irresistible itty-bitty creations, made out of shimmering glass beads on delicate wire. They are created following simple patterns and using the technique of threading the wire back and forth

Metal & Wire

Tools for the job

✿ eyelets
✿ Anywhere hole punch
✿ setting tool
✿ hammer
✿ self-healing mat

Eyelets

These handy little embellishments have a multitude of applications. Traditionally used on clothing, bags and tents, eyelets have diversified to become a papercrafter's best friend

One of the most versatile embellishments, eyelets are perfect for attaching elements to cards such as tags and vellum. They allow movement and dimension, and can be used to thread ribbons, to add a decorative element on a page or as binding.

There are many colours, shapes and finishes available. Snaps are eyelets without the hole, and metal plaques are another popular form. In addition, there's a selection of shapes and letters that can be threaded onto the eyelet prior to it being set onto the paper or cardstock.

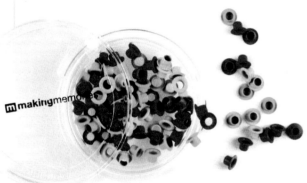

makingmemories

Laced Boot
by Natalie O'Shea

Materials:

☐ mink-coloured cardstock
☐ lilac velvet cardstock
☐ lilac thread
☐ Making Memories eyelets
☐ Buttons Galore purple flowers
☐ Boot template (from Templates section)

To create:

1. Cut out the boot from the mink cardstock, using the template. Fold over on the fold line with a bone folder.
2. Trace the top and heel of the template onto the velvet card. Cut these out and adhere them to the boot.
3. Punch holes and set eyelets down the front of the boot, and thread with the lilac thread, attaching it to the rear with tape.
4. Adhere the two buttons to the boot to embellish.

i Eyelets are decorative metal fasteners designed for paper and fabrics. A cylinder made from aluminium, one end is rolled over and flattened out. An eyelet is passed through a hole in the item that you want to join to your project, then the reverse of the eyelet is flattened out using a setting tool and a hammer, creating a secure fitting

step 1
To set an eyelet you need a hammer, a setter and a hole punch to match the size of your eyelet. If you're using the Anywhere hole punch, you'll also need something to protect the surface of your desk – a self-healing cutting mat is ideal.

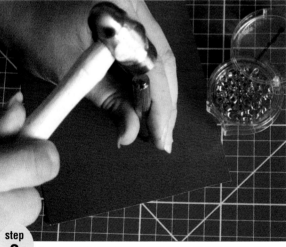

step 2
To start, make a hole using your Anywhere hole punch. This punch has a round, hollow tip at one end that cuts a hole through the paper. Place this sharp edge where you want the hole to be, then tap with your hammer. If you're using a thicker card or multiple layers, you may need to give it a couple of taps.

Congratulations

by Emma Amor

Materials:

- ☐ cream card blank
- ☐ Making Memories ribbon
- ☐ vellum
- ☐ Making Memories eyelets

To create:

1. Print out a black and white picture of a baby onto white paper. Trim to size.
2. Cut a piece of vellum the same size. Attach the vellum and the picture together with the small eyelets.
3. Secure this to the centre of the card and finish with a piece of Congratulations ribbon.

With Love

by Delphy Tuson

Materials:

- ☐ rustic metal heart
- ☐ safety pin
- ☐ Making Memories eyelets
- ☐ rickrack, gingham & organza ribbons
- ☐ Prism red cardstock
- ☐ Paper Adventures red gingham paper
- ☐ Hero Arts alphabet stamps
- ☐ black StāzOn inkpad
- ☐ card blank

To create:

1. Cover the front of the card blank with the gingham paper. Punch or cut out a square of the red cardstock.
2. Stamp your message onto the organza ribbon using the StāzOn ink. Attach the ribbon with two eyelets, so that it looks like a tag.
3. Attach the heart with foam tabs, and tie gingham ribbon to the safety pin. Secure the pin to the cardstock.
4. Adhere the red square to the card and finish the card off with the rickrack.

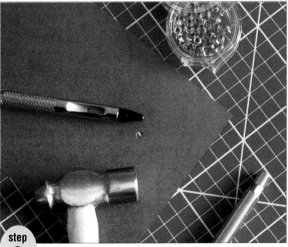

step 3 *Once you've made the hole, insert the eyelet through it so the nice rounded edge is on the front of your project. Carefully turn the project over, holding the eyelet in place, and position it onto a self-healing mat.*

step 4 *Place the setting tool against the straight end of the eyelet. Tap the end of the tool with a hammer. A few short taps (rather than one big smash) is recommended. Once the back has splayed out and flattened, give it a gentle tap with the flat end of the hammer – this helps to reduce sharp edges.*

Oh Christmas Tree
by Susan McCourt

Materials:
- ☐ cream corrugated card blank
- ☐ red & green velvet paper
- ☐ Making Memories Christmas Tree eyelet charm
- ☐ Prism cream cardstock
- ☐ corner punch

To create:

1. Cut a 5x5cm square from the green velvet paper. Cut a 4x4cm square from the cream cardstock, and a 3.5x3.5cm square from the red velvet paper.

2. Using the corner punch, shape the edges of the velvet squares. Attach the eyelet charm to the centre of the red square.

3. Build up the squares using foam tabs, and attach them to the front of the card.

Cool Yule
by Emma Reid

Materials:
- ☐ patterned papers
- ☐ Making Memories pink eyelet snaps
- ☐ Prism brown cardstock
- ☐ Ranger Walnut Distress inkpad
- ☐ card blank
- ☐ silver star confetti

To create:

1. Cut a triangle from the green patterned paper and ink the edges. Attach eyelet snaps randomly across the piece, positioning one at the top with the confetti star.

2. Cut and ink a background from patterned paper, and a small rectangle from brown cardstock for the trunk.

3. Attach all the elements to the card, fixing the triangle on with foam pads for added dimension.

Sweet Love
by Christi Snow

Materials:
- ☐ Colorbök Little People patterned paper
- ☐ loopy eyelets
- ☐ Rhonna Farrer Romantic Dreamy epoxy sticker
- ☐ Prism Sky Blue & Brick Red cardstock
- ☐ fibres

To create:
1. Trim the patterned paper and mount it onto the card.

2. Arrange the loopy eyelets so that they form a symmetrical zigzag, and run the fibres through the loops.
3. Finish off with a bow and the epoxy stickers.

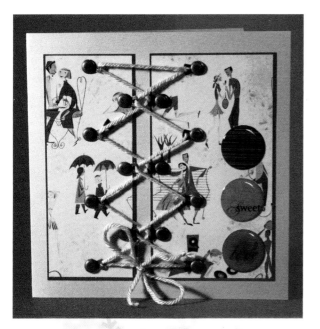

Tropical Smile
by Trish Latimer

Materials:
- ☐ Prism red, orange, black & pink cardstock
- ☐ pink, gold, red & orange paper
- ☐ orange eyelets
- ☐ pink brads
- ☐ Ting tag punch
- ☐ gold thread
- ☐ Mod Podge
- ☐ alphabet stamps
- ☐ large daisy stamp

To create:
1. Stamp a daisy three times onto pink cardstock, cut them out and attach three eyelets to the centre of each.
2. Tear fragments of pink, gold, orange and red paper, and adhere to a card panel. Cover with Mod Podge to add sheen.
3. When dry, matt the card panel onto black cardstock then wrap it with gold thread. Punch five tiny tags from orange cardstock, and stamp the letters to form the word 'smile'.
4. Attach the tags to the torn paper panel with hot pink brads. Adhere the panel to a red card blank, and the three daisies to the panel.

For more details on manufacturers and distributors, turn to page 158

Tools for the job

✿ wire jig
✿ wire writer
✿ wire
✿ various seed beads
✿ template (see Template section)

Wire words & shapes

Creating a customised shape or greeting in wire couldn't be easier. We show you how to get started

There are two ways to create wire words and shapes: one is with a jig, which is a relatively inexpensive item; the other is with a pegboard that can be set to a template that the wire is woven around. The latter is made easier if you use a wire writer, a pen that dispenses the wire, and enables you to make the wire nice and taut.

If you don't have a wire jig, you could use long-nosed pliers and a drawn or printed template.

Your desired shape or word has to be drawn or printed onto paper first, and this is then used as a template.

Thank You
by Kirsty Wiseman

To create:

1 Either by using the jig or shaping by hand, create the metal shape. Stitch the seed beads following the shape of a heart onto an offcut of fabric.

2 Tear the edge of the card, inking the edges. Cut three squares from the papers and punch a circle. Take the circle and ink the edges.

3 Cut a strip of paper and attach it to the outside edge of the inside so that it shows behind the torn edge.

4 Attach all the various pieces of paper and embellishments and finish off with a greeting made with a Dymo.

Materials:
☐ offcuts of co-ordinating patterned papers
☐ blue seed beads
☐ wire
☐ Dymo & black tape
☐ card blank
☐ Adirondack blue inkpad
☐ adhesive gem shapes
☐ button
☐ needle, thread & offcut of material

ⓘ **Wire words and shapes are made by bending, curling and shaping wire into letters or an object. They are often embellished with beads**

step 1 *Write or print your chosen word (in this case, 'Love') onto a piece of paper. Experiment with different fonts and methods of joining your letters. Try to keep your pen on the paper as you write the word. Some fonts that are ideal for wire words are CK Cursive, Mistral, Rage Italic and Synchronous. All of these can be downloaded from the Internet.*

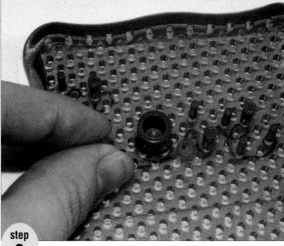

step 2 *Place your word under the wire jig and use it as reference to fix differing sizes of pegs in the jig and form the varying loops, curls and angles within your word. You can buy a word jig from as little as £5, or you could make one with a piece of wood, nails and screws. Children's pegboards can be customised to work.*

Materials:
- ☐ cream card blank
- ☐ cream luggage label tag
- ☐ copper wire
- ☐ cream ribbon
- ☐ wooden beads
- ☐ handmade papers
- ☐ Ranger Vintage Photo Distress inkpad
- ☐ Anna Griffin Butterfly stamp

To create:

1. Stamp the butterfly background onto the cream card blank and tag. Ink the edges of the tag.

2. Make a heart shape from the wire, leaving a long tail to thread the beads onto. Twist the wire around a small paintbrush to create a spring effect, tucking the end into the last wooden bead.

3. Glue the heart shape onto handmade paper. Once dry, cut around the heart.

4. Attach the label with foam tabs and tie a ribbon to the heart embellishment and the tag. Finally, fix the heart to the card using foam tabs and Glue Dots.

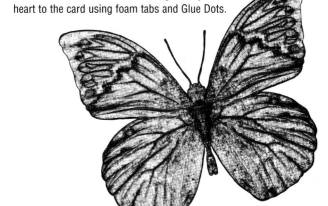

Wire Heart Butterflies
by Andrea Miller

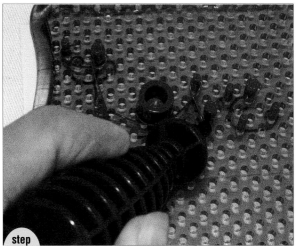

step 3 *Using your wire writer, hold the end of the wire and begin to form you word. Wrap the wire around the pegs and ensure that the tension of the wire is taut at all times. Once you've gone all the way along the word, snip the wire.*

step 4 *You can then lift the design from the wire jig – it's easy to misshape the word beyond repair at this point, so be careful. You can tweak and reshape your word with tweezers and fingers.*

Wish
by Barbara Mercer

Materials:
- ☐ wire
- ☐ pearl beads
- ☐ seed beads
- ☐ Making Memories flower brads
- ☐ Making Memories ribbon
- ☐ Making Memories exPRESSions
- ☐ D-rings
- ☐ Scrapworks 12x12 patterned paper
- ☐ FIMO
- ☐ Amoco Moons & Words Push Mold
- ☐ card blank

To create:

1 Adhere paper, patterned side up. Cut a strip of paper, fold as shown, and attach a D-ring. Then fix into place with a brad.

2 Cut a curved corner of paper and fold the tip up as shown. Attach a D-ring, then fix the tip into place with two brads.

3 Make the dragonfly by looping wire to form the wings, wrapping it around at the point where they meet and leaving a length for the antenna. Take a second length of wire to form the second antenna then wrap the wire around the wings. Create a body by threading with beads.

Green Oriental
by Trish Latimer

Materials:
- ☐ Prism green cardstock
- ☐ green vellum
- ☐ Oriental background paper
- ☐ bamboo skewer
- ☐ gold Krylon pen
- ☐ gold wire
- ☐ purple & green seed beads
- ☐ tiny eyelets
- ☐ sealing wax
- ☐ Oriental coin
- ☐ Oriental Lady stamp
- ☐ purple ink

To create:

1 Tear the edges of a vellum panel and stamp the lady onto this in purple ink. Tear the edges of a background panel and place on top of a green card blank. Place the vellum panel on top of this.

2 Adhere the panels to the card blank using four tiny eyelets. Drip sealing wax onto one corner then press a coin into it.

3 Colour a length of bamboo skewer with gold Krylon pen. Leave to dry, then wrap with gold wire.

4 At intervals, thread purple and green seed beads onto the wire. Attach the wired skewer to the card blank by threading more gold wire through the holes made by the tiny eyelets, and twist to secure.

Anniversary
by Lousette Ashton

Materials:
- ☐ sei Granny's Kitchen patterned paper
- ☐ Prism blue & cream cardstock
- ☐ wire
- ☐ Papermania wire word
- ☐ seed beads
- ☐ Ranger Walnut Distress inkpad
- ☐ silver thread
- ☐ silver embossing foil
- ☐ card blank
- ☐ Making Memories brads

To create:

1 Glue a strip of blue cardstock towards the bottom of the card blank. Cover the front of the card with patterned paper that has a strip torn out of the bottom third so that the blue cardstock will show through.

2 Attach the wire word to this blue strip using brads. Cut a circle from silver embossing foil and another slightly larger one from blue cardstock.

3 Edge the blue circle with brown ink. Shape a piece of thick craft wire into a 3D heart and attach to the metal circle. Layer the circles together and finish off with a small tag.

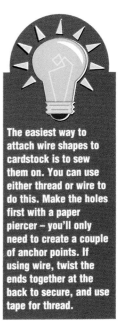

The easiest way to attach wire shapes to cardstock is to sew them on. You can use either thread or wire to do this. Make the holes first with a paper piercer – you'll only need to create a couple of anchor points. If using wire, twist the ends together at the back to secure, and use tape for thread.

Tools for the job

✿ needle
✿ thread
✿ paper piercer

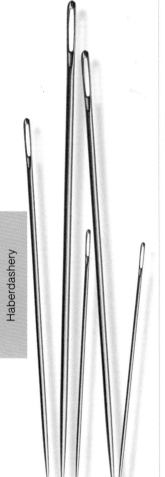

Hand stitching

Anyone who can thread a needle can sew on paper. It is easy, and adds lots of texture. It is also a great way of attaching elements to your cards

There are no specialist tools or techniques for stitching paper, although a few helpful hints and tricks may help you on your way. The biggest potential frustration is that paper doesn't self-heal when you push the needle through in the wrong place, leaving a nastily visible mistake. This can be resolved by piercing the holes for your stitch work with a paper piercer or a needle that has had the blunt end pushed into a cork.

Almost any thread can be used, and any size needle – a finer finish is achieved when you use a smaller needle. You can buy templates and tools that will help you create more intricate and specialist designs, but these are not essential.

Friends by Christi Snow

Materials
☐ DCWV The Paper Stack: Matchmakers 2
☐ Making Memories Moxie Fab Alphabets Cool stickers
☐ Making Memories Friendships Artistic Tags
☐ navy cardstock
☐ string

To create:
1 Cut varying lengths of co-ordinating patterned papers. Mount onto the front of the card.
2 Attach the alphabet stickers at the base of these strips.
3 Hand-stitch the edges of these stickers.
4 Attach the Friends tags to finish.

step 1 *Pierce the stitching pattern in the paper, ideally working on a self-healing craft mat or pricking mat.*

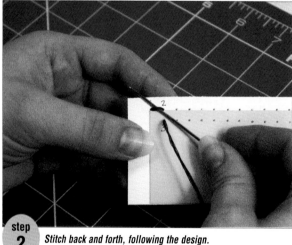

step 2 *Stitch back and forth, following the design.*

Dream a Little Dream
by Trish Latimer

Materials
- ☐ white cotton fabric
- ☐ image transfer paper
- ☐ black fabric ink
- ☐ white cardstock
- ☐ black cardstock
- ☐ red embroidery floss
- ☐ needle
- ☐ pricking mat
- ☐ face stamp
- ☐ alphabet stamps

To create:

1 Stamp the face onto card then transfer onto white cotton, using the image-transfer paper. Adhere to a cut-to-size piece of white cardstock, folding over two edges neatly and fraying the remaining two edges.

2 Hand-sew around the two neat edges. Stamp the word 'Dream' onto the cotton, adhere onto cut-to-size white card, and fray all four edges.

3 Hand-sew French knots in the corners. Prick holes along the sides of a black card blank, and, using the holes as your guide, hand-sew a zigzag and blanket stitch to the edges.

4 Adhere the two stamped panels to the card blank.

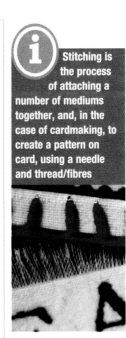

Stitching is the process of attaching a number of mediums together, and, in the case of cardmaking, to create a pattern on card, using a needle and thread/fibres

Haberdashery

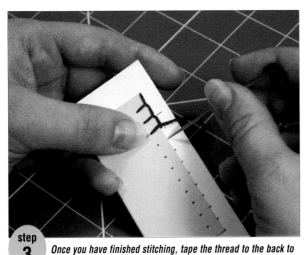

step 3 *Once you have finished stitching, tape the thread to the back to hold it.*

For a bold hand-stitched effect, use an embroidery needle with a big eye to sew thicker thread. Be sure to wear a thimble though as the needlepoint is very sharp

Tools for the job

✿ needle
✿ thread
✿ paper piercer
✿ shank remover
✿ buttons
✿ ribbons
✿ hole punch

Haberdashery

Buttons & bows

The humble button and ribbon started out as a way of fastening garments. Over recent years, they have been liberated and take centre stage as embellishments on cards

There are so many beautiful embellishments that can be purchased for your papercrafts, but why not try raiding the sewing box for some inspiring ideas. There is such a huge choice of colours, styles and sizes of buttons and ribbon that you will be sure to find the right one to match your project.

Buttons will add that perfect texture to your cards at negligible cost, and they can be attached easily with glue, a Pop Dot or stitching. They also make a great fastener on a more unusual card or tag book. Ribbons are extremely versatile and will add a texture and dimension to your

cards that is impossible to imitate with papers. They can be attached as bows with glue, threaded through holes, tied through holes, or short pieces can be folded over and stapled onto your cards for a contemporary look.

A rummage in the sewing box is sure to unearth many other treasures suitable for use in your cardmaking. A number of manufacturers have recognised the haberdashery trend and have replicated it through embellishments, stickers and stamps. Although these come in a fantastically varied range, there's nothing like using the real thing.

BOY by Teresa Collins

Materials
☐ My Mind's Eye Wild Asparagus patterned paper
☐ Junkitz Manila tags & Boy label
☐ ribbon
☐ fabric
☐ Junkitz assorted buttons
☐ Making Memories staples

To create:

1 Ink the edges of the manila tag and decorate the base with staples.

2 Using more staples, affix the boy label to some patterned paper with inked edges then attach this to some material, allowing the paper and material to overlap. Glue these to the tag.

3 Tie a length of ribbon through the hole on the tag. Glue a piece of ribbon to the lower part of the tag. Tie short lengths of cord through three buttons and glue these into place on the ribbon.

step 1 *Thread your cotton through the button and tie on the top, trimming the loose ends. Using a Pop Dot or 3D foam pad on the reverse of the button, attach it to the card.*

step 2 *Punch a number of holes into the edge of your card, using either a standard stationary hole punch or an anywhere punch.*

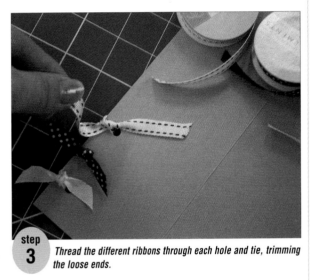

step 3 *Thread the different ribbons through each hole and tie, trimming the loose ends.*

Tag Card by Kirsty Wiseman

Materials
- [ ] cream card blank
- [ ] Prism green, orange and plum cardstocks
- [ ] various ribbons
- [ ] various buttons
- [ ] material
- [ ] Tag template (see Template pages)
- [ ] daisy punch

To create:

1 Cover the bottom of your card with floral material – it is a good idea to use a Xyron, if you have one, to adhere the material. Punch out some flowers and attach these to the material.

2 Secure a strip of plum cardstock at the top of the fabric to hide the join. Attach three co-ordinating buttons.

3 Tie ribbons around the edge of the aperture. Position a piece of green cardstock behind the aperture then, onto this, stick a library card and tag that have been made using the template. Decorate with ribbons and a punched-out daisy.

Haberdashery

Haberdashery

Best Friends by Louise Gilmour

Materials

- ☐ card blank
- ☐ Bazzill Basics textured cardstock
- ☐ Shabby Princess patterned paper
- ☐ Anne Keenan Higgins stamp
- ☐ Marvy Le Plume pens
- ☐ white pigment inkpad
- ☐ necklace pendant
- ☐ grosgrain ribbon
- ☐ sequins
- ☐ rickrack
- ☐ zip

To create:

1 Cut a piece of patterned paper to fit the bottom third of the card. Cut the blue cardstock to fit the remainder of the card.

2 Stamp, emboss, colour-in using the Marvy markers and cut out. Attach to the card using 3D foam pads. Fix the embellishment to the zipper before securing to the join in the cardstock and patterned paper with double-sided tape. Glue sequins and rickrack on top.

3 Round the corners of the card, and soften the edges with a white inkpad using the direct-to-paper technique. Apply the ribbon tab to the reverse of the card.

You will find that many decorative buttons come with a shank or loop on the reverse. These can be removed with a shank remover or pair of nail clippers, but do be careful as the shank can fly off

Thank You by Katie Shanahan-Jones

Materials

- ☐ various fabric scraps
- ☐ Creek Bank rickrack tape
- ☐ Gin-X patterned papers
- ☐ StāzOn ink
- ☐ Doodlebug stitched ribbon
- ☐ Hero Arts clear buttons & stamps
- ☐ ribbon slider

To create:

1 Cut a piece of cream fabric slightly smaller than your card and fray the edges. This is the base of the design.

2 Cut various fabrics into different-sized rectangles and layer onto the cream background. Hold them in place with a small piece of double-sided tape then stitch around them with white cotton.

3 Stick rickrack tape and ribbons across the piece again with double-sided tape. Stamp onto clear buttons with StāzOn ink and stitch in place.

4 Stick the finished piece onto a white card using double-sided tape.

Materials

- [ ] patterned paper
- [ ] Making Memories shaped clip
- [ ] various buttons
- [ ] pink cardstock
- [ ] eyelets
- [ ] fabric stickers
- [ ] ribbons
- [ ] embossing inkpad
- [ ] black embossing powder

Love by Carol Monks

To create:

1 Score and fold patterned paper to form the base of your card. Stick velvet ribbon across the top of the checked design. Adhere the main fabric sticker, chalking the edges to soften.

2 Stamp the words onto the grosgrain ribbon and heat-emboss the words using black embossing powder. Attach this with various eyelets.

3 Attach the shaped clip, add a tag and embellish with a sticker and buttons.

> A button is a small disc-shaped attachment typically used on clothes. They are made from an extremely wide range of materials, including bone, ivory, metal, plastic and wood. Buttons were first used by the Ancient Romans, and are now often used for decorative effect only, without a practical function

Birthday Bear by Louise Gilmour

Materials

- [ ] Paper Mill Shop cardstocks
- [ ] Sizzix Earth Tones patterned papers
- [ ] embroidered motif
- [ ] Making Memories eyelets
- [ ] twill
- [ ] sheer ribbon
- [ ] brown pigment inkpad
- [ ] computer

To create:

1 Score and fold cardstock. Cover with two different patterned papers. Ink around the edges of the lighter patterned piece. Machine-stitch around this.

2 Fix eyelets along the spine of the card, and thread the sheer ribbon through these. Tie, and trim off the loose ends.

3 Using a PC, design a word strip in a variety of fonts and print onto twill tape. 'Age' the twill by toasting it with a heat gun. Adhere to the card then stick on the embroidered teddy.

Tools for the job

- ✿ paper
- ✿ thread
- ✿ sewing machine
- ✿ tape
- ✿ scissors

Machine Stitching

Crazy-stitched Dill
by Trish Latimer

Materials:

- ☐ green & white cardstocks
- ☐ Adirondack Oregano dye re-inker
- ☐ Marvy Le Plume green, yellow & maroon pens
- ☐ sewing machine
- ☐ ribbon
- ☐ Real Dill stamp

To create:

1 Make a colourwash using water and drops of the re-inker, and wash over a white cardstock panel. Colour the stamp using the Marvy pens, and spritz water onto it.

2 Stamp onto the colourwashed panel. Matt onto a complementary green panel. Using the sewing machine, randomly stitch around the flower. Take a green card blank and cut a small strip from the front, so it is narrower than the back.

3 Machine-stitch down the exposed back of the card. Adhere the stitched panel to the front and add a ribbon to finish.

Stitching is becoming more commonplace on cards, with cardmakers searching for a more professional look to their designs. So dust off that sewing machine for a more consistent stitch

There was a time when all sewing was done by hand. Most early attempts at machines tried to replicate hand stitches, and were generally a failure. Then, in the 1700s, various inventors came up with different stitches to suit a mechanical machine. Hundreds of designs, rows and patents later we have what we know now as the domestic sewing machine. It has a variety of sized and styled stitches, and some models even embroider. You can buy specialist small machines designed specifically for use with paper, although your ordinary sewing machine can be used effectively. So, it's time to grab your machine from the back of the cupboard and add it to your cardmaking arsenal!

Most cottons and threads can be used to stitch paper; you will need to test the stitch on the paper first, just as you would test the tension on a scrap of fabric. You can also stitch without any thread, which will leave a fine, detailed pierced edge and can add a unique look to your cards. The biggest problem that you will face when stitching paper or card is that it is no way forgiving, so use the theory of measure twice, stitch once – you get the idea. Secure your loose threads on the reverse of the projects with tape.

step 1 *Position the patterned papers onto the front of your card and adhere to your base card.*

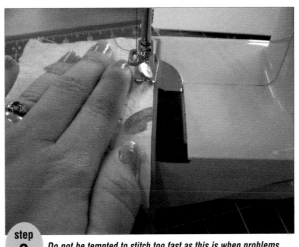

step 2 *Place the card under the foot of the sewing machine and lower the foot. Stitch as you would with paper.*

Wedding Card by Sharon Neill

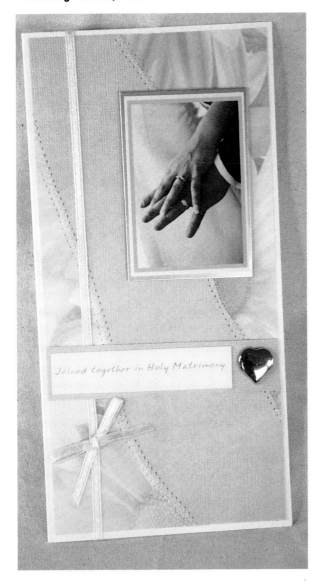

Joined together in Holy Matrimony

step 3 *Do not be tempted to stitch too fast as this is when problems occur. Cut the thread when you get to the end and fasten the loose ends down with tape.*

Materials:
- [ ] white textured cardstock
- [ ] Frances Mayer floral paper
- [ ] silver cardstock
- [ ] Bazzill Blossom cardstock
- [ ] cream ribbon
- [ ] computer-generated image
- [ ] metal embellishments

To create:

1. Cut, score and fold the textured cardstock to use as the base of your card. Cut a piece of the floral paper to fit on the card, leaving a border around it.

2. Cut the Bazzill cardstock and fit it diagonally across the floral paper. Sew in a zigzag along the edges of the Bazzill cardstock using cream threads. Attach this piece to your base card.

3. Print out the computer-generated image, matt onto silver cardstock and fix to the card using 3D pads.

4. Attach the ribbon and bow down the side of the card, print the title onto white cardstock and matt onto the Bazzill. Finish by attaching the metal embellishment.

Flower Pot
by Katie Shanahan-Jones

Materials:
- ☐ Hero Arts stamps
- ☐ pigment inks
- ☐ clear embossing powder
- ☐ cardstock

To create:

1 Cut the vase and leaves from cardstock. Use a straight stitch on the sewing machine along the middle of the leaves, and sew back and forth across the vase. Pull the loose threads through and secure on the back of the piece with tape to stop them pulling out.

2 Cut a piece of dark blue cardstock slightly smaller than the blank card. Sew a looped line of stitching in light thread for the butterfly trail. Ink the flower stamp with pigment inks, stamp onto white cardstock and emboss with clear embossing powder.

3 Cut out the flowers and mount onto the card as shown. Use foam tape to raise up the flower. Cut a butterfly and stick at the end of the line of stitching.

Pram by Lousette Ashton

Materials:
- ☐ cardstock
- ☐ varied ribbons
- ☐ embroidered pram embellishment

To create:

1 Cut and score your cardstock to the size of the required card.

2 Adhere two strips of ribbon across the front of the card. Stitch over these with different-sized stitches and using various colours of threads.

3 Finish off by adhering the pram.

Haberdashery

Treasure Love
by Teresa Collins

Materials:
- ☐ Junkitz Boy Stars patterned paper
- ☐ Li'l Davis Designs chipboard tag & patterned paper
- ☐ Junkitz Tim Holtz safety pin
- ☐ ribbon & lace
- ☐ Autumn Leaves Foofabet letters
- ☐ various fabrics

To create:
1. Glue the Foofabet letters onto various materials and affix to the lower edge of the card.
2. Glue a strip of patterned paper into position in the top third of your card. Machine-stitch a length of ribbon to create a one-off design and tie through a hole punched at the top of your card.
3. Tie a length of material through the chipboard tag. Attach this to the card by threading a large safety pin through both of the knots in your material and ribbon. Glue the tag into position.

ⓘ Sewing machines make a stitch, called a sewing-machine stitch, usually using two threads, although machines do exist that use one, three, four or more threads. Sewing machines can create a great variety of plain or patterned stitches. They include means for gripping, supporting and conveying the fabric past the sewing needle to form the stitch pattern

Haberdashery

Do not set the stitch too small, as all this will do is perforate your paper

Embellishments

ATCs are so small that decorating them can be difficult and often requires a lot of thought. Your box of oddments and offcuts is the perfect place to start. The following list should give you some ideas of what you could use:

● *torn papers & vellum*
● *newspaper*
● *sheet music*
● *images of all kinds*
● *stamped offcuts*
● *almost anything metal*
● *buttons*
● *gems*
● *lace*
● *ribbons*

Be Happy by Teresa Collins

ATCs

Artist Trading Cards, more commonly referred to as ATCs, have come a long way since they were first suggested in 1996 by Swiss artist Vanci Stirnemann. Originally intended as greetings to be swapped between fellow artists face to face, they've become a medium for many an online swap

Cafe Du Monde by Christi Snow

Old as the Hills
by Sonya Montgomery

Piller to Post
by Sonya Montgomery

To create:

1. Start with a card, be it a playing card or a card cut to size.
2. Prepare your background: this can be painted (acrylics are ideal) or made from paper.
3. Add your main image.
4. Add embellishments – as many or as few as you like or as works for the piece.

Build up an ATC box and keep it to hand. Use it to store any offcuts from your cardmaking, striking images you come across in magazines, and bits and bobs of interesting embellishments. When you're looking for inspiration, dive into your box – you'll be amazed at the findings

Not only are they great for swapping with fellow addicts, but they're equally as valuable as miniature works of art for your pleasure and that of others. If you're stuck for inspiration and can't stand the idea of making a full-size card, why not have a go at creating some ATCs?

There are only two 'rules' with ATCs: the first is the size, which should be 3.5x2.5" – no more, no less. The second rule is that they should be swapped, not sold. Well, who says? We'll start off by ignoring half the rules!

You'll find that you're using the same skills for ATCs as

for larger greetings cards. The only difference, which may take a little mind adjustment, is choosing the correct size of images. Large items can swamp the small canvas on which you're working for ATCS, but trial and error will soon reveal what works for you, and you'll steam ahead!

ATCs are highly addictive and you may find it difficult to make just one at a time. So instead, create a whole series of cards to a chosen theme – Birthday, Wedding, Christmas and Anniversary ATCs all make ideal card toppers, and are excellent to have as standbys for those last-minute, 'oh dear, I forgot' emergencies.

Celebrate!

This first section of galleries is devoted to those special occasions that are cause for a good old knees-up, a celebratory cheer or maybe a romantic dinner for two

ADULT BIRTHDAYS

Birthday Wishes
by Natalie O'Shea

Embossed Wild Rose
by Jane Tarrant

Materials:
- ☐ pale lavender scored & folded card
- ☐ clear embossing inkpad
- ☐ Obsidian Violet embossing powder
- ☐ small silver peel-off greeting
- ☐ Moonglow pinks & purples palette
- ☐ purple angel hair
- ☐ silver mirror card for matting
- ☐ Magenta 20031.17 Wild Rose panel stamp

To create:

1. Stamp and emboss the blossom on purple card with Obsidian Violet embossing powder.

2. Colour in the flowers using purple/pink Moonglow pigments mixed with a little Gum Arabic (or PVA glue) and water.

3. Trim and layer with purple angel hair and silver mirror card onto a lavender card, then add your chosen greeting.

Materials:
- ☐ Prism plain or textured green & pink cardstocks
- ☐ sei Aunt Gerti's Garden patterned paper
- ☐ sei buttons
- ☐ Lasting Impressions green stitching thread
- ☐ Making Memories Jelly Greeting
- ☐ Li'l Davis wooden flowers & stitching template

To create:

1. Use the back of one of the patterned papers to create a square pink base card.

2. Tear two corners from one of the pieces of patterned paper and attach to the top-right and bottom-left corners.

3. Attach a wooden flower to the bottom-right and top-left corners of the card, and a green button to the centres using a wet adhesive.

4. Tear a rectangle of the pink spotty paper and mount onto a rectangle of green card.

5. Affix your jelly greeting to the central panel then stick this to the centre of the card.

6. Using your template, pierce holes to the top-left and bottom-right corners of the greeting panel, and use green thread to join the holes with straight stitches.

Happy Birthday
by Natalie O'Shea

Materials:
- ☐ Prism plain or textured green & pink cardstocks
- ☐ sei Aunt Gerti's Garden patterned paper
- ☐ sei brads & buttons
- ☐ Lasting Impressions pink stitching thread
- ☐ Making Memories Jelly Greeting & leather flower
- ☐ Li'l Davis stitching template

To create:

1. Use the back of one of the patterned papers to create a rectangular green base card.
2. Tear the bottom of a piece of the striped patterned paper and attach to the top of the card.
3. Cut a rectangle of the large spotty patterned paper and mount onto some pink card leaving a small border. Mount again onto plain green card leaving a larger border, and once more onto pink card, leaving a small border.
4. Attach a jelly greeting to the top-left internal panel and three rhinestone brads to the bottom-right corner of the panel. Fix the whole panel to the right-hand side of the card.
5. Tie some thread through the holes of a brown button, knot and trim. Attach the button to the centre of a pink leather flower and attach the flower into the top-right corner of the card.
6. Use the template and some pink thread to produce the spiral pattern to the left-hand side of the card.

Ribbon Weave
by Clair Simmons

Materials:
- ☐ folded card
- ☐ white card
- ☐ wavy ribbon
- ☐ The Eyelet Outlet Happy Birthday tag
- ☐ Daisy peel-offs
- ☐ cotton cord
- ☐ Sticky Fingers lilac, light blue and pink dye
- ☐ Xyron

To create:

1. Dip two of each length of wavy ribbon in the dyes (two pink, two light blue and two lilac) and set aside to dry.
2. Paint the white card with light blue dye and dip the white cord in as well.
3. Once dry, run the lengths of ribbon through the Xyron and attach in a criss-cross pattern to the white card.
4. Stick the daisy peel-off in the lower right-hand corner and punch a hole in the centre of it.
5. String the Happy Birthday metal tag onto the cord, thread it through the daisy and attach the cord with tape.
6. Stick the square to the card with foam pads and one on the back of the metal tag.

Lavender Card
by Susan Hobb

Materials:
- ☐ Hot Off The Press Icy Rainbow Creative pack, Birthday Card Quotes, Accent Birthday Embossed Focals, Ribbon Sentiments, Accents Antique & Pewter mini brads
- ☐ white cardstock
- ☐ Craf-T chalks

To create:

1 Cut the card into a 5" square, then cover the card front with blue stamp pad paper. Cut apart the ribbon sentiment and glue one 'Happy Birthday' sentiment to the centre of each side of the card front, even the outer edges.

2 Punch eight squares from lavender diagonally striped paper and fold into kites as shown.

3 Glue the edges, then matt onto lavender vellum. Glue two kites to each other as shown, overlapping the ribbon edges.

4 Cut out the embossed focal and lightly chalk it lavender. Fold a small piece of ribbon and glue to the back of the focal, extending from the top.

5 Adhere the focal to the centre of the card with foam tape and finish with a brad. Add brads to each of the outer corners of the tea bag kites.

6 Cover the inside with lavender diagonally striped paper. Cut out the quote and matt onto lavender vellum. Fold a small piece of ribbon and glue to the back of the quote, extending above it. Adhere to the centre of the inside.

50th Birthday
by Nura Karpowitsch

Materials:
- ☐ cream textured card
- ☐ ColorBox bronze inkpad
- ☐ Fiskars brayer background handle & brayer background mesh roller
- ☐ Impex card topper
- ☐ 3D foam pads
- ☐ gold holographic Birthday peel-off
- ☐ gold number peel-off

To create:

1 Fold the cream textured card in half to make your card.

2 Attach the Fiskars mesh roller to the Fiskars brayer handle, then ink the mesh roller with the bronze inkpad.

3 Roll the Fiskars handle with inked mesh roller over the length of the cream card.

4 Cut the Impex card topper to your desired size, then ink around the edges of the cream part of the topper with the bronze inkpad.

5 Attach the card topper with 3D foam pads centrally onto the top two thirds of the base card.

6 Now attach the 'Happy Birthday' and '50' peel-off centrally to the bottom third of the card.

Three Leaves
by Kay Carley

Materials:
- ☐ Pébéo Vitrea 160 frosted glass paints in Cloud, Blue & Lemon
- ☐ Pébéo Vitrea 160 Transparent Outliner in Pewter
- ☐ acetate
- ☐ Françoise Collection Silver Leaves peel-offs
- ☐ Art Impressions F-2055 Branches stamp
- ☐ Magenta B-0219 Swirl stamp
- ☐ Moonglow Iridescent Brights set
- ☐ VersaMark inkpad
- ☐ plain white card
- ☐ dark blue vellum
- ☐ sponge wedge
- ☐ paintbrushes
- ☐ JudiKins Color Duster
- ☐ 'Happy Birthday' metal word plaque
- ☐ Fiskars All-in-One ¹⁄₁₆" hole punch & eyelet setter
- ☐ eyelet mat
- ☐ Sakura white glaze pen
- ☐ Bazzill Arctic monochromatic brads
- ☐ crystal glitter
- ☐ old tile (for mixing paints)

Happy 18th Birthday
by Nura Karpowitsch

Materials:
- ☐ bronze card
- ☐ cream textured card
- ☐ Magic Mesh fine-weave copper mesh
- ☐ beige 7mm ribbon
- ☐ 3D foam pads
- ☐ gold number peel-off
- ☐ gold letter peel-off
- ☐ Savvy Stamps mesh stamp
- ☐ ColorBox bronze pigment inkpad

To create:

1 Pour a small amount of Frosted Cloud onto a tile and sponge all over a panel of acetate. Once dried arrange three of the peel-off leaves onto a piece of white card and slide them under the acetate. Trace over the leaves with the pewter outliner and set aside to dry. Mix a little of the Frosted Blue with the white paint on an old tile, then brush it onto the leaves. Add yellow paint to the middle leaf. Leave to dry then colour the background squares with the white glaze pen and sprinkle on crystal glitter. Set aside to dry again.

2 Randomly stamp the branches onto the front of a 14.5x14.5cm plain white card using the VersaMark. First dab Cerulean Blue from the Iridescent Brights set onto the stamped branches with an old paintbrush, then Starbright Green Blue, swirling both powders into the images then into the card. Brush off any excess with the Color Duster. On a strip of dark blue vellum repeatedly stamp the swirl using the VersaMark. Dab Cerulean Blue onto the swirls then brush off the excess.

3 Tear both edges of the vellum strip, wrap vertically around the square card close to the left-hand side, and tape to the inside. When the leaves have dried, attach the acetate panel to the card by placing it onto the front and punching a hole in each corner with the Fiskars punch, ensuring it goes through both the acetate and the card. Insert a dark blue brad into each hole, bending the prongs back on the inside to secure. Attach the word plaque.

To create:

1 Fold the bronze card in half to make the base of the card. Cut the cream textured card to size. Cut a 12cm length of the copper mesh and trim to a width of 19 whole squares. Cut three 12cm lengths of ribbon.

2 Weave the ribbon through the mesh, snipping an opening after every fourth row. Alternate the weave with each strip. Attach the ribbon to the edge of the cream card, along the shortest side. Secure the ribbon and mesh with sticky tape.

3 Use the mesh stamp with the bronze inkpad to add detail. On a piece of cream card, apply the 'Happy 18th Birthday' peel-off. Mount the cream card onto a piece of bronze card. Using 3D foam pads, stick this onto the mesh stamped area at an angle, then attach the cream card to the bronze card.

Ruby Angel
by Jane Tarrant

Materials:
☐ JudiKins Angel 2452H stamp
☐ A Stamp in the Hand Field of Sky stamp
☐ white deckle-edged card
☐ clear acetate
☐ black StäzOn
☐ gold Brilliance inkpad
☐ piece of thin gold card
☐ ruby & cranberry inks
☐ silver Luna Lights or glass paint
☐ white crumpled tissue paper
☐ glitter/sprinkles
☐ Diamond Glaze

To create:

1. Stamp the JudiKins Angel carefully onto a piece of acetate using black StäzOn. Do not press too hard as it might slip.
2. Squeeze five 5p-piece-sized blobs of Diamond Glaze onto the back of the stamped acetate when dry.
3. Squeeze out a small drop of each coloured ink. Dust with glitter or sprinkles.

4. Spread the coloured glue using your finger or a piece of crumpled paper. Cover with a piece of white tissue or mulberry paper.
5. Leave to dry then trim with a paper cutter.
6. Cut a rectangle of thick gold paper about 1.5cm larger than the acetate. Punch decorative corners and slide in the acetate. (A small dab of glue will help the centre to lay flat.)
7. Stamp the Field of Sky stamp around the edge of the white folded card using the gold Brilliance inkpad.
8. Add a stamped or peel-off greeting and a red cord or ribbon on the spine.

Flowers & Frills
by Karen Watson

Materials:
☐ A4 textured white card
☐ A4 purple card
☐ A4 white glossy card
☐ Stamp-It patterned paper
☐ Kaleidacolor Berry Blaze inkpad
☐ StäzOn black inkpad
☐ Impression Obsession Leopard Nightie E6335 & Rose Pump D6400 stamps
☐ Woodware medium flower punch
☐ Scrap-Ease Happy Birthday rub-ons
☐ 3mm crystals & Kandi Kane applicator (optional)
☐ brayer

To create:

1. Brayer a piece of glossy white card with Berry Blaze ink. Once dried, cut a piece to 9x10cm and, using the black StäzOn, stamp the Leopard Nightie onto it. Cut another piece to 8x5cm and stamp the Rose Pump onto it with black ink. Cut a strip of brayered card big enough to stick your rub-on words onto. Punch out two pink and two purple flowers.
2. Cut a piece of printed paper to measure 18x12cm. Layer onto a piece of purple card and cut an even border all around. Take your A4 piece of white card and fold in half. Use double-sided tape to glue the panel onto the card.
3. Arrange the stamped pieces of card as shown, sticking the Nightie down with double-sided tape, and the shoe, flowers and wording with foam pads.

Celebrate

CHILDREN'S BIRTHDAYS

Tied Birthday Boy
by Mandy Anderson

Materials:
- ☐ sei Serendipity patterned paper and alphabet stickers
- ☐ Scrapbook Sally cardstock
- ☐ Making Memories tags and Celery ribbon
- ☐ Making Memories Simply Stated Heidi rub-ons
- ☐ Memories Pale Olive chalk inkpad

To create:
1. Trim the cardstock to make a rectangle.
2. Ink the edges and attach the rectangle to a folded card.
3. Apply the rub-ons to the card.
4. Stick the alphabet letters onto the square tags.
5. Punch a hole on the opposite edge of each tag, then tie them together with fibre.
6. Attach the tags to the cardstock rectangle.

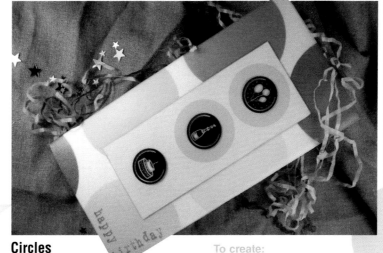

Circles
by Mandy Anderson

Materials:
- ☐ sei Serendipity vellum and frames
- ☐ Making Memories Rummage stamps
- ☐ Memories Pale Olive chalk inkpad
- ☐ Tango Twirl Birthday paperclips

To create:
1. Stamp the words 'happy birthday' onto the bottom right-hand side of a folded card.
2. Attach the vellum to the card.
3. Ink the edges of the frame and place it over the vellum.
4. Attach the paperclips to the middle of the circles.

Celebrate

Girly Girl
by Christi Snow

Materials:
- ☐ Making Memories Coastline Beach Towel patterned card
- ☐ Hero Arts Friendly Greetings stamp set
- ☐ Thinkable Inkables Ooolala
- ☐ StäzOn black ink
- ☐ VersaMark inkpad
- ☐ white and black card
- ☐ white embossing powder
- ☐ jewellery-making supplies

To create:

1. String some beads together on some beading thread to make the bracelet charm.
2. On the Beach Towel paper, draw a gentle curve almost the width of the card. Trim and mount onto white card leaving a narrow border showing. Attach to the base card.
3. Punch two holes at the top, bottom and middle of the curve, so that they measure the same distance apart as the width of the bracelet.
4. Thread a ribbon through each of the sets of holes and tie on the bracelet.
5. White-emboss the Birthday saying in the lower-left corner.
6. Stamp the Girly Girl sideways in the top-right corner.

Zach Birthday
by Teresa Collins

Materials:
- ☐ Junkitz Earth Floral patterned paper
- ☐ Junkitz Birthday Zipper Pullz
- ☐ Junkitz Tim Holtz Safety Pinz
- ☐ library card
- ☐ May Arts ribbons
- ☐ Making Memories chipboard letters
- ☐ Ranger Tim Holtz Walnut Stain Distressed & Van Dyk Brown inkpads
- ☐ Hero Arts stamp

To create:

1. Cover the libary card with a piece of patterned paper slightly smaller than the card. Stitch ribbon over this.
2. Select your title or name and cut squares from co-ordinating paper scraps. Use various scissors to give variety, and ink the edges of the squares. Stick these down and arrange the chipboard letters.
3. Embellish the card with rickrack and various other tags and stamps.

Dragonfly Dreams
by Karen Watson

Materials:
- ☐ A4 white textured card
- ☐ glossy white card
- ☐ purple card
- ☐ Kaleidacolor Berry Blaze inkpad
- ☐ VersaMark inkpad
- ☐ Stampendous Stamps Dotted Dragonfly F092, Small Dot Dragonfly C145 & Birthday Dots L126 stamps
- ☐ Woodware medium flower punch & Southwest corner punch
- ☐ silver embroidery thread
- ☐ 3mm crystals
- ☐ brayer

To create:

1 Cut a strip of glossy white card to measure 15x5cm. Ink the Birthday Dots stamp with the VersaMark and stamp onto the top and bottom of the strip. Leave for a few minutes while the ink dries, then gently wipe over the top with a soft cloth or tissue.

2 Ink your roller with Berry Blaze then brayer over the strip of glossy card. Repeat until you have a strong even colour. You will find that the Berry Blaze will not have touched the VersaMark stamped image and the pattern will show through clearly.

3 Take your A4 sheet of white card, cut to measure 15x29.7cm and fold in half. Use the smaller dragonfly stamp and the Berry Blaze inkpad to randomly stamp the background. Glue the panel you made in step 1 to the centre of the card with double-sided tape.

4 Take a 6.5cm square piece of glossy card. Use VersaMark to stamp the larger dragonfly then follow the instructions in steps 1 & 2 to create a 'resisted' dragonfly. Mount this onto a piece of purple card and cut an even border all around. Punch the corners with the Southwest corner punch and wrap some silver embroidery thread through the indents. Mount this panel onto the card with foam pads.

5 Finish off the card by using foam pads to attach a punched flower to each corner of the centre panel as shown, and apply a crystal to the large dragonfly and also to the centre of each flower.

Wishing
by Christi Snow

Materials:
- ☐ white, black and red cardstocks
- ☐ Non Sequitor Stamps Scrabble Alphabet
- ☐ Inkadinkado Swirly stamp
- ☐ red & black inkpads
- ☐ gingham ribbon
- ☐ craft sponge

To create:

1 Take a piece of white card. Lay a piece of copier paper down one side (at a slight angle and about one third of the way over) and sponge on some red ink. Place your paper on top of the line that you just sponged and sponge on black ink in the opposite direction until you have a modified tic-tac-toe board.

2 Stamp random images within the sections using scrap paper to mask any areas where you do not want the images to flow over. Layer onto red cardstock, leaving a small border showing.

3 Mount onto the card base. Finish off by tying a ribbon around the spine of the card.

Celebrate

Motorbike
by Kay Carley

Materials:
- ☐ plain white card & black card
- ☐ ivory pearlescent card
- ☐ Chubbies 40 wax crayons from The Early Learning Centre
- ☐ Aspects of Design stamp set 10 – Men's
- ☐ Brilliance pearlescent yellow inkpad
- ☐ Cat's Eyes pigment inkpad set
- ☐ Something Special embossing powder set
- ☐ Françoise Gold Friendly Phrases peel-offs

To create:

1 Make a wax crayon background as shown using the ivory pearlescent card and gold and white crayons. Create a tall, folded black card and trim the ivory wax crayon backgrounds to fit the front.

2 Stamp the map stamp with the black Cat's Eye inkpad a couple of times onto white card, re-inking between each impression. Tear a thick strip wide enough for the motorbike image to fit onto and cut a thinner strip for the bottom of the card, tearing the top edge. Lightly ink the edges.

3 Layer the bigger white strip onto a thicker black panel. Cut a black strip of card slightly thicker than the smaller white strip, so that the black shows only along the top edge, and attach them to the card as shown.

4 Using the motorbike stamp and black Cat's Eye inkpad, stamp onto white card. Emboss with clear embossing powder. Apply colour to the image with the Brilliance yellow inkpad, the red and black inkpads and moist cotton buds. Cut out leaving a narrow border. Mount to the prepared panels with Sticky Fixers.

5 Place one of the gold peel-off greetings onto a piece of black card and trim. Mount to the card with Sticky Fixers.

Cupcake by Katie Shanahan-Jones

Materials:
- ☐ Anita's square cards
- ☐ Making Memories pink cardstock
- ☐ Making Memories Express It magnetic stamps
- ☐ VersaMark inkpads
- ☐ ultrafine crystal glitter
- ☐ Colorbök Perfect Cards kit

To create:

1 Use a 5x5" cream card and stick double-sided tape around all four edges. Peel off the protective paper and sprinkle the tape with superfine white glitter.

2 Cut a piece of pink cardstock measuring 3.5x3.5" and go around the edges with a punch or with scissors. Ink around the edges with dark pink or mauve ink.

3 Use white ink to stamp 'Happy Birthday' all over the pink card. Overlap the edges of the card too.

4 Stick the pink card in the middle of the cream card.

5 Take the cupcake embellishment from the Perfect Cards kit and mount on foam tape. Stick it in the centre of the pink cardstock.

Celebrate

Flower Girl
by Katie Shanahan-Jones

Materials:
- ☐ Cloud 9 Design paper
- ☐ Cloud 8 Design page coaster
- ☐ Dymo label maker
- ☐ Making Memories blossoms
- ☐ small buttons
- ☐ pink diamantés

To create:

1 Take a Baby Girl-themed Cloud 9 Design page coaster and sand around the edges with a piece of rough sandpaper to give white edges.

2 Stick the page coaster onto the right-hand side of your card. Using Glue Dots, stick the blossoms onto the left-hand side of the card – odd numbers of blossoms look best. Make sure you use a blossom on the page coaster to cover the word 'Baby', unless of course your card is for a baby girl.

3 Using a Dymo machine, make a tape saying 'Birthday' and stick it onto the card next to the page coaster. If you don't have a Dymo then use alphabet stamps or a computer.

4 Stick a button in the middle of each blossom – wet glue such as Diamond Glaze works well.

5 For a little girlie glitz, add some small diamante stickers onto the card.

Ladybirds
by Katie Shanahan-Jones

Materials:
- ☐ QuicKutz Ladybird DoubleKutz
- ☐ QuicKutz mosaic tile
- ☐ spotted ribbon
- ☐ Making Memories cardstock tags
- ☐ Bazzill cardstock
- ☐ Making Memories foam stamps

To create:

1 Tear a piece of black cardstock so it's slightly smaller than the card, and stick it to a red card.

2 Using double-sided tape, stick a length of spotty ribbon lengthways across the bottom third of the card.

3 Cut out three squares in cream cardstock using your QuicKutz or a 1" punch, then stick them to the card as shown.

4 Use foam number stamps to print a white '3' in the centre of the card, then emboss it with white embossing powder. This makes the number slightly raised against the black cardstock.

5 Cut three ladybird bodies from black cardstock and stick one in the centre of each cream square.

6 Cut three ladybird wings from red cardstock and stick one over each body section.

7 Use a Dymo machine to print 'Happy Birthday' on a tape, then stick it to the top left-hand side of the card.

8 Attach a small tag to the ribbon using a tiny safety pin.

Celebrate

ANNIVERSARY

Lavender
by Gina Martin

Materials:
- ☐ white hammer card
- ☐ blue card
- ☐ Art Impressions Salvia stamp
- ☐ Rubbadubbadoo Happy, Anniversary – Stick 'n' Stamp
- ☐ Marvy Le Plume II Jungle Green, Steel Blue, Sepia & Prussian Blue pens

To create:

1 Colour only the flower part of the stamp using Prussian Blue, and stamp between 10 and 12 times with one inking, changing position each time to create depth in the flowers. Repeat this step a further two times.

2 Using the thin end of the Jungle Green pen, draw in the stems of the flowers, remembering to draw outwards towards the bottom of the spray. Using the thin end of the Sepia pen, draw across the flower spray where the stems begin to move outwards. Draw two loose ends each side of the tie to create the loose strings.

3 Punch the corners of the blue card with the Southwest corner punch and attach to the white card with double-sided tape. Then attach the mounted picture to the base card with more tape. Colour the word stamps with the Steel Blue pen and stamp onto the bottom of the card.

Wisteria
by Gina Martin

Materials:
- ☐ white hammer card
- ☐ No.3 watercolour paintbrush
- ☐ Art Impressions Left Blue Bird, Tall Flower & Large Ivy stamp
- ☐ Rubbadubbadoo May Your Day stamp
- ☐ Marvy Le Plume II Jungle Green & Steel Blue pens

To create:

1 Colour the words on the May Your Day stamp with the Steel Blue pen, and stamp onto the lower right-hand side of the card. Colour the Large Ivy stamp with the Jungle Green pen and, starting at the bottom left-hand corner, begin to stamp the wisteria vine. Ink after every two impressions, then carry on up to the top of the card and along. Stop when the vine is just over the verse.

2 Using the same stamp and pen, add branches to the main stem, stopping when you like the shape. Colour the top third of the Tall Flower stamp with the Steel Blue pen. Next, turn the stamp upside down, so the point of the flower is facing downwards. Add the flower to the vine, stamping five times per inking to add depth to the plant.

3 Ink the Blue Bird with Steel Blue and stamp just above the verse. Dip the paintbrush into the water and squeeze almost all of the water out. Finally, pull the colour from the Blue Bird stamped image into the middle, but remember to leave his breast clear.

Love Tokens
by Wendy Vane

Materials:
- ☐ cream card & copper linen card
- ☐ plum paper
- ☐ bronze VersaColor inkpad
- ☐ Doodlebug Design Inc red heart tokens
- ☐ Hero Arts Happy Anniversary rubberstamp
- ☐ double-sided tape
- ☐ wet glue (that dries clear, eg Diamond Glaze)
- ☐ 18-gauge copper coloured wire
- ☐ wire cutters & pliers

To create:

1 Use the cream card to make your card base. Ink the edges of the card using the bronze inkpad.

2 Cut an 11.5cm square of plum paper. Stamp 'Happy Anniversary' onto it using the bronze inkpad to create the background, and ink the edges. Stick to the middle of the cream card.

3 Cut a rectangle 4x12cm from copper card and stick onto the middle of the card vertically.

4 Cut a 5x6cm rectangle from plum paper. Ink the edges with bronze and attach onto copper card.

5 Cut 25cm of wire and bend it in half. Thread the heart token onto the wire so it rests in the bend. Twist the wire twice to secure the token then follow the template design using pliers.

6 Glue the wire heart onto the plum paper, allowing the heart token to dangle over the copper card.

Ivy Leaves
by Gina Martin

Materials:
- ☐ white hammer card
- ☐ No.3 watercolour paintbrush
- ☐ Art Impressions Large Ivy, Large Foliage, Watering Can & Buds stamps
- ☐ Rubbadubbadoo Happy, Wedding, Anniversary – Stick 'n' Stamp
- ☐ Marvy Le Plume II Jungle Green, Steel Blue & Sepia pens

To create:

1 Colour the Watering Can stamp with the Steel Blue pen and stamp onto the card. Wet a No. 3 watercolour paintbrush then squeeze out almost all of the water. Pull the colour from the stamped image into the watering can, leaving the centre of all rounded parts clear. This gives the can a rounded shape.

2 You will need to dip your brush into the water and squeeze it out three or four times. Ink the Large Foliage stamp with the Jungle Green pen and stamp onto the opening of the watering can. Repeat once more, this time placing the Large Foliage stamp just touching the top of the previously stamped foliage image.

3 Colour the Large Ivy stamp with the Jungle Green pen and position around the stamped foliage until you like the finished result (about nine times should suffice). Ink the Buds stamp with the Steel Blue pen and add the flowers amongst the foliage.

4 'Sit' the watering can onto the paper by using a colour wash. Draw some Steel Blue pen onto your palette and add a little of the Sepia. Using a very wet brush, mix the two colours together on your palette – the more water you use, the weaker the colour. Brush the wash under the watering can image, working from right to left, to create a shadow.

5 Arrange the word stamps onto the magnetic block and colour with the Steel Blue pen. Stamp on the right-hand side of the card.

Flower Stand
by Gina Martin

Materials:
- ☐ No.3 watercolour paintbrush
- ☐ white hammer card
- ☐ blue card
- ☐ blue ribbon
- ☐ Art Impressions Plant Stand, Small Flowerpot, Large Ivy, Large Foliage, Tall Flower, Grass Clump & Blue Bird Right stamps
- ☐ Marvy Le Plume II Jungle Green, Steel Blue & Sepia pens

Garden Scene
by Gina Martin

Materials:
- ☐ white hammer card
- ☐ No.3 watercolour paintbrush
- ☐ blue card
- ☐ Art Impressions Gate, Salvia, Leaves, Large Ivy, Grass Clump, Pebbles & Bird Trio stamps
- ☐ Rubbadubbadoo Wishing you a, Happy, Anniversary – Stick 'n' Stamp
- ☐ Marvy Le Plume II Jungle Green, Steel Blue, Pine Green & Sepia pens

To create:

1 Ink the Garden Gate with the Sepia pen and stamp onto the card. With a nearly dry brush, pull the colour into the gate. Colour the Leaves stamp with the Jungle Green pen first, then over-ink in places with the Pine Green pen. Using the two colours on the stamp helps to create light and depth. Stamp out three times with one inking each side of the gate image.

2 Colour the Large Ivy stamp with the Jungle Green pen and stamp out nine branches above the hedge on the left of the gate, inking each time. Colour the flower part of the Salvia stamp with the Prussian Blue pen. Stamp out 10 flowers, with one inking of the stamp, above the hedge of the right side of the gate image. Then colour the stamp again and make another 10 impressions.

3 Ink the bottom half of the Grass Clump stamp with the Jungle Green pen and stamp each side of the stamped gate image and along the bottom of the hedge. Stamp two lots of Pebbles, and the Bird Trio with the Sepia pen. Pull the colour into the centre with a nearly dry brush.

4 Arrange the word stamps on the magnetic block and colour with the Steel Blue pen. Stamp onto a separate piece of card. Punch the corners of the picture and the words with the Southwest corner punch. Attach the picture to the left-hand side of your card with double-sided tape. Finally, set the greeting at an angle at the bottom-right corner with foam tape, as shown.

To create:

1 Ink the Plant Stand and Small Flower Pot with Sepia and stamp onto the card as shown. Pull the colour with a nearly dry brush. Leave some white areas to give the impression of a rounded shape. Colour the Large Foliage with Jungle Green and stamp above the image of the flowerpots. Colour Large Ivy with Jungle Green and stamp some hanging down and two pointing upwards.

2 Colour the top third of the Tall Flower with Steel Blue. Turn the stamp upside down so the point is down and then stamp onto the ivy. Draw in chains with the thin end of the Sepia pen. Colour the lower half of the Grass Clump with Jungle Green and stamp three times around the base of the plant stand. Colour the Blue Bird Right with Steel Blue and sit him on one arm of the plant stand. Colour him in with a nearly dry brush.

3 Mount the picture onto blue card. Lay a strip of double-sided tape down the middle of the card. Fix some thin blue ribbon to this strip and attach the whole picture using foam tape. Make a ribbon bow at the top and stamp the sentiment at the bottom of the card, either side of the ribbon.

Celebrate

Hugs & Kisses
by Clair Simmons

Materials:
- ☐ white card
- ☐ Pixie Press vellum
- ☐ Hot Off The Press sticky ribbons
- ☐ jewelled heart
- ☐ mini peel-off messages
- ☐ Xyron 510
- ☐ Diamond Glaze

To create:

1 Make a 75x203mm white card. Run the vellum through the Xyron and affix it to the card.

2 Edge the vellum with a length of sticky ribbon.

3 Affix the jewelled heart using Diamond Glaze then add your desired message.

All Wrapped Up
by Wendy Vane

Materials:
- ☐ orange, brown & copper effect paper/card
- ☐ cream card
- ☐ orange vellum
- ☐ orange & gold inkpads
- ☐ VersaMark inkpad
- ☐ double-sided tape
- ☐ Happy Anniversary rubberstamp by Hero Arts
- ☐ Love rubberstamp by Savvystamps
- ☐ Impex 34-gauge gold beading wire
- ☐ deckle-edged scissors

To create:

1 Fold some cream card to make your card base. Ink around the edges of the heart with the orange inkpad.

2 Cut a piece of linen copper card measuring 11.5x10.5cm and attach to the top middle of the card. Leave a gap at the bottom for your greeting. Stamp 'Happy Anniversary' in the middle bottom of your cream card using the orange inkpad.

3 Cut a 10.5cm square from the brown card and tear a small strip from the edges to give the feathered edge. Always tear towards you. Attach this to the centre of the copper card.

4 Cut a 10.5cm square from the orange vellum and again, tear a small strip from the edges to give the feathered edge. Attach this to the centre of the brown card. Make sure you put the tape where it won't be seen.

5 Cut a 8.5cm square from the orange card. Using the 'Love' stamp and a watermark inkpad, stamp the card repeatedly with the greeting. Tear a small strip from the edges to give a feathered effect. Attach this to the centre of the orange vellum.

6 Using the template as a guide, cut out the heart shape from another piece of cream card using the deckle-edged scissors. Ink the edges of the heart with the gold inkpad.

7 Put double-sided tape on the back of the heart to stick down the beginning of the wire. Wrap the wire around the heart in various directions until you are happy that the card is covered to your satisfaction. Finish the wire at the back of the heart and stick down using double-sided tape. Attach the heart to the centre of the orange card.

Celebrate

Water Pump
by Gina Martin

Materials:
- ☐ white hammer card
- ☐ No.3 watercolour paintbrush green card
- ☐ green card
- ☐ green & white ribbon
- ☐ Art Impressions Water Pump stamp
- ☐ Rubbadubbadoo Happy, Anniversary – Stick 'n' Stamp
- ☐ Marvy Le Plume II Jungle Green, Steel Blue & Sepia pens

Romantic Roses
by Jane Tarrant

Materials:
- ☐ Rubber Stampede Romantic Roses Large Bouquet stamps A1563G
- ☐ backing paper with pale yellow base colour
- ☐ A4 ivory linen card
- ☐ yellow & green marker pens
- ☐ white Pearl Ex (optional)
- ☐ scraps of black & copper card for layering
- ☐ copper wire
- ☐ bronze, white & yellow beads
- ☐ Southwest corner punch
- ☐ large square punch
- ☐ 'waste' peel-off squares

To create:

1 Colour the pump and well of the Water Pump stamp with the Sepia pen. Use the Steel Blue pen to colour the bucket and use the Jungle Green pen for the grass. Stamp onto white hammer card.

2 Dip a No. 3 watercolour brush into water and squeeze out almost all of the water. Pull the colour in each part, leaving some white parts to make highlights, as this helps to create a roundness to the picture. Clean the brush in water before working on a differently coloured part of the picture.

3 Mount the cards together as shown, using double-sided tape.

4 Lay a strip of double-sided tape 2.5cm from the bottom of the card and stick the ribbon onto it. Colour the Happy Anniversary stamp with the Jungle Green pen and stamp onto the right-hand side of the card.

To create:

1 Make a pale yellow backing card by adding a little white paint to a yellow ochre basecoat.

2 Stamp the large rose bouquet and colour in with marker pens. Scribble colours onto a white tile and blend with a small amount of white Pearl Ex to give a pearlescent sheen to the colours.

3 Punch out three squares randomly from the coloured and glazed image.

4 Cut three black squares and three copper squares, each a little bigger than the previous layer. Punch out the corners of the black card using the Southwest corner punch.

5 Glue the layers together then wrap with a length of copper wire to which has been added 12 tiny beads. Let the beads slide down three at a time with each twist of the wire, keeping them at the front.

6 Secure the beaded wire to the back of the card with double-sided tape. Glue the pieces diagonally onto a slim cream card and decorate with some tiny peel-off squares.

CONGRATULATIONS

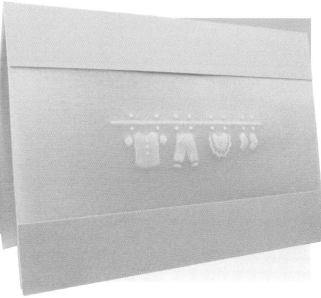

Congratulations, a son
by Mieke Sprenger

Materials:
- ☐ Pergamano embossing pad deluxe, embossing tool (extra-fine ball) and free embossing tool (large ball)
- ☐ white pencil
- ☐ Perga spray
- ☐ white paper
- ☐ Ice Blue Fantasy parchment
- ☐ ordinary parchment paper
- ☐ Baby template

To create:

1 Attach a sheet of ordinary parchment paper onto the pattern with removable tape. Trace the folding line and card outline with white pencil. Remove the clothesline from the Baby template and place it on the parchment paper.

2 Turn the parchment paper and emboss the contours of the clothesline with the extra-fine-ball tool. Emboss the whole template with the large-ball tool.

3 Carefully remove the template from the parchment paper. Emboss some details – like the trouser pockets, turned-over sock and the dots on the bib – on the under side with the extra-fine-ball tool.

4 Cut the outer card to size and fold. Attach a sheet of white copying paper behind a sheet of Ice Blue Fantasy parchment with Perga spray. Cut out two strips measuring 17.5x3cm from this sheet.

5 Attach these strips onto the front of the outer card with Perga spray. Cut the inner card to size and attach it inside the outer card with double-sided tape.

Congratulations, a daughter
by Mieke Sprenger

Materials:
- ☐ Pergamano embossing pad deluxe, embossing tool (extra-fine ball) and free embossing tool (large ball)
- ☐ white pencil
- ☐ Perga spray
- ☐ salmon pink & white Fantasy parchment
- ☐ Duck and Dummy templates
- ☐ dabbing brushes
- ☐ white & skin-coloured Pintura
- ☐ pink paper

To create:

1 Attach a piece of white Fantasy parchment onto the pattern. Place the self-adhesive duck template on the parchment paper.

2 Dip the dry brush straight in the Pintura, so that about 1–2mm of the brush picks it up. Dab the duck with the brush.

3 Clean the brush and dab the second layer of the duck with skin-coloured Pintura. Dab the wings and eye with white Pintura. Repeat these three steps for the dummy. Use the self-adhesive dummy template.

4 Attach a sheet of white copying paper with Perga spray behind the white Fantasy parchment, where you dabbed the duck and dummy. Cut these extra fronts to size.

5 Cut the first and third extra front sheets to size. Attach them onto the front of the outer card with Perga spray. Cut the inner card to size and attach it inside the outer card with double-sided tape.

Celebrate

You're a Star
by Dyan Reaveley

Materials:
- [ ] black card
- [ ] black shrink plastic
- [ ] gold Krylon pen
- [ ] VersaMark pad
- [ ] A Stamp In The Hand Writing stamp N-1772
- [ ] black Brilliance inkpad
- [ ] gold UTEE
- [ ] gold wire
- [ ] foam squares

To create:

1 Take a piece of card, fold it in half and put it to one side.

2 Draw the large star shape onto black shrink plastic. Cut out and shrink. Punch three star shapes from black shrink plastic and shrink. Ink the writing stamp with black Brilliance pad and put to one side.

3 Ink all four star shapes with a VersaMark pad and cover with gold UTEE. Heat the powder to melt and, whilst hot, cover with more gold powder. Heat again and whilst hot, stamp over the shapes with the writing stamp. Leave to cool then remove the stamp.

4 Take a piece of black card and edge with a gold Krylon pen. Attach to the black folded card. Coil some wire into desired shapes and attach to card. Put foam squares onto the back of the stars and stick on top of the wire.

5 Write 'Well Done' onto a piece of black shrink plastic using a gold Krylon pen. Shrink, flatten and attach to your card using a foam square.

Exam Congratulations
by Dyan Reaveley

Materials:
- [ ] white and red card
- [ ] black and white shrink plastic
- [ ] A Stamp In The Hand Background Text N-1772 stamp
- [ ] black StäzOn ink
- [ ] black tassel
- [ ] red ribbon
- [ ] black eyelets
- [ ] foam squares

To create:

1 Cut and score a card, then fold in half to form your base card and put to one side.

2 Cut a square out of black shrink plastic and punch a hole in the middle. Shrink and flatten. Attach the tassel through the hole.

3 Cut a square of white shrink plastic. Ink up the writing stamp with black StäzOn and stamp the plastic all over. Shrink, and whilst hot, roll up into a scroll shape and leave to cool. Then tie a piece of red ribbon around it.

4 Take a square of white card and edge with black StäzOn ink. Stamp writing diagonally and attach to a red square using black eyelets. Edge with black ink.

5 Take the folded card and stamp writing across it diagonally. Attach red and white card centrally.

6 Attach foam squares to the scroll and mortar board, then fix to the centre of the card.

Celebrate

Stork
by Kay Carley

Materials:
- white-gold pearlescent card
- plain white card
- Baby Blue fine-weave Magic Mesh
- Hero Arts E1875 Shadow Stamp III
- Woodware Craft Collection/ Françoise Collection FRK001 New Baby stamp
- Pebbles Inc. set of pastel chalks
- VersaMark inkpad
- Sticky Fingers Ice Blue and Pearl Sparkle
- Buttons Galore pack of Stork buttons
- wire cutters
- small heart punch
- scrap paper

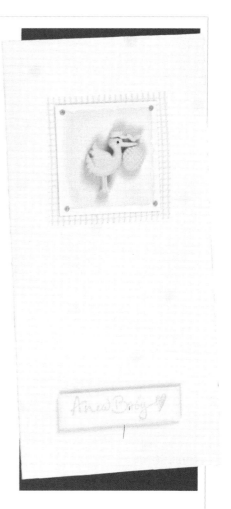

To create:

1 Punch a heart from a piece of scrap paper and, using the heart aperture/negative that you have created on the piece of paper, randomly chalk blue hearts through the paper onto a tall white-gold pearlescent card. Stamp the shadow stamp onto white card using the VersaMark inkpad and apply the lighter shade of yellow chalk to the entire square using a swirling motion, then apply blue chalk to the edges of the square. Trim to size and add Ice Blue Sparkle dots to the corners.

2 Stamp the wording onto white card using the VersaMark inkpad and apply blue chalk to the impression with a dabbing motion. Trim to size and chalk the edges with yellow. Apply Pearl Sparkle to the heart.

3 Remove the shank from the back of the button with wire cutters and stick the button back together with Wonder Tape. Mount centrally to the chalked square with 3D pads. Cut a square of the Magic Mesh and adhere to the card. Adhere the stork square over the mesh and mount the wording near to the bottom of the card.

Tied Scroll
by Clair Simmons

Materials:
- cream, red and white cardstocks
- red and gold threads
- gold embossing powder & embossing inkpad
- Making Memories Providence magnetic stamps
- straight narrow gold peel-off borders
- double-sided tape

To create:

1 Fold a sheet of cream cardstock in half to make an 88x120mm card. Affix a piece of red card onto the front, leaving a border as shown.

2 Roll white card around a pencil to create a scroll, then tie this with red and gold thread. Stick the scroll to the card with Glue Dots.

3 Using the magnetic stamp, create your desired words then stamp and emboss them in gold.

4 Edge the red card with the narrow gold peel-off borders.

Celebrate

Good News
by Clair Simmons

Materials:
- ☐ lilac, coral and white cardstocks
- ☐ Penny Black Good News stamp
- ☐ Pebbles Inc. I kan'dee pastel chalks
- ☐ Making Memories Providence magnetic stamps
- ☐ purple inkpad
- ☐ embossing ink and black powder
- ☐ double-sided tape
- ☐ foam pads

To create:
1. Fold a sheet of lilac cardstock in half to make a 105x141mm card. Use sticky tape to fix the coral card to the top centre of the lilac card.
2. Stamp the image onto white card and emboss it in black. Then chalk the image to colour.
3. Stick it to the centre of the coral card with foam stamps.
4. Using the magnetic stamps, create your message and stamp it in purple.

Congratulations
by Clair Simmons

Materials:
- ☐ white leather-effect card
- ☐ red card 115x115mm
- ☐ large gold star
- ☐ Hero Arts Congratulations stamp
- ☐ embossing ink and gold powder
- ☐ star peel-offs
- ☐ double-sided tape
- ☐ foam pads

To create:
1. Fold the white card in half. Stamp 'Congratulations' around each edge of the red card, then heat-emboss the words with gold powder.
2. Tape the red card to the centre of the white card.
3. Attach the gold star to the middle of the red card with foam pads.
4. Finally, stick star peel-offs in each corner of the red card.

Celebrate

Graduation
by Clair Simmons

Materials:
- ☐ red marbled card
- ☐ cream card 114x97mm
- ☐ Jolee's Boutique Graduation stickers
- ☐ double-sided sticky tape
- ☐ narrow gold border peel-offs
- ☐ small Congratulations peel-offs

To create:

1 Fold the red marbled card in half.

2 Tape the cream card to the middle of the red card.

3 Apply the cap and gown stickers and the 'Congratulations' peel-offs to the cream card.

4 Attach gold border peel-offs to the edge of the cream card. Finally, create the border around the red card as shown.

Graduation Tag
by Clair Simmons

Materials:
- ☐ purple marbled card
- ☐ 450mm of gold fibre
- ☐ navy blue card
- ☐ Deluxe Cuts 2-T tag template
- ☐ Jolee's Boutique Graduation stickers
- ☐ Congratulations peel-offs
- ☐ foam pads
- ☐ masking tape
- ☐ two gold eyelets

To create:

1 Fold the purple card in half. Use the gold fibre to make a cross on the left-hand side of the card as shown, then stick it down. Tie shorter lengths of gold fibre to the cross.

2 Using the template, cut two tags from the navy card, then set the gold eyelets on the tags.

3 Apply the Jolee's stickers to one tag, and the peel-off message of your choice to the other.

4 Use foam pads to stick the tags to the card.

Celebrate

Wedding & Christmas

Traditionally in the spring or summer, the 'big day' of a friend or relative is always deserving of a special handmade card to add that personal touch to your message of congratulations. Then to cheer us up in the darker winter days, the festive season provides the perfect opportunity to use some bright colours and sparkle while you wish everybody you know a very merry Yuletide

WEDDING

Chalked Hearts
by Cath Allen

Materials:
- ☐ white cardstock
- ☐ Deluxe Designs Natural deluxe chalks
- ☐ Hero Arts Decorative Heart stamps
- ☐ Archival Ice Blue Brilliance Pearlescent inkpad
- ☐ blue vellum

To create:

1. Using a small piece of cloth, chalk a piece of white card with blue and purple chalk and stamp out the heart designs.

2. With the example as a guide, cut out the hearts and stick them onto the card with double-sided sticky foam.

3. Write 'Wedding' with black pen onto the blue vellum and cut it out.

4. Stick the word onto the bottom-right corner of the card.

Ringing Bells
by Cath Allen

Materials:
- ☐ white cardstock
- ☐ bell-shape cutter
- ☐ Ranger Purple Rain Beadazzles
- ☐ silver pen

To create:

1. Cut out two bells and stick them onto the centre of the white card using double-sided foam.

2. Randomly stick the silver hexagon shapes from the Beadazzles around the bells.

3. Draw a pencil line and write 'Wedding' with the silver pen on the card.

4. Leave the ink to dry, then rub out the pencil line.

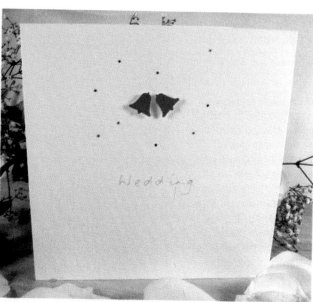

Shaker Hearts
by Cath Allen

Materials:
- [ ] white card
- [ ] turquoise velvet card
- [ ] peel-offs
- [ ] metal confetti
- [ ] black Profipen 0.1 (edding 1800)
- [ ] double-sided foam
- [ ] double-sided tape
- [ ] transparencies
- [ ] heart template

To create:
1. Use white cardstock as the base for your card. Using the bone folder, score the card and fold.
2. Cut a heart out of the turquoise velvet card. Draw a second heart inside the one already cut out by measuring 1.25cm from the edge and cut this one out using the craft knife.
3. Using the heart template, cut the acetate in the same way. Stick double-sided tape to the back of the heart frame and adhere the acetate to it. Putting the turquoise heart downwards on the table and acetate uppermost, stick double-sided foam onto the acetate. Make sure there are no gaps and press down firmly.
4. Place some metallic confetti into a neat pile on the white card and place the turquoise heart on top. Ensuring no confetti is under the foam, press firmly.
5. Stick the rose peel-offs onto the turquoise velvet card and cut out. Place a double-sided foam square on the reverse and stick onto each corner of the white base card.
6. Using a pencil, rule a line under the heart and, with the black pen, write 'wedding invitation'. Let the ink dry and rub out the pencil line.

Wedding Invite
by Cath Allen

Materials:
- [ ] pink card measuring 27x13.5cm
- [ ] purple chalk
- [ ] Hero Arts Heart stamp
- [ ] Penny Black Letter background stamp & Alphabet stamps
- [ ] VersaColor Amethyst inkpad
- [ ] purple ribbon
- [ ] diamantés

To create:
1. Score and fold the pink card, and chalk the right-hand side of the card using the eye shadow applicator and purple chalk.
2. Stamp the chalked part of the card with the letter background using the amethyst inkpad, referring to the example as a guide. Add your two hearts and your 'Wedding Invite' wording.
3. Stick the ribbon down the left-hand side of the card using double-sided tape, and glue the diamantés down the ribbon, ensuring an even space between each one.

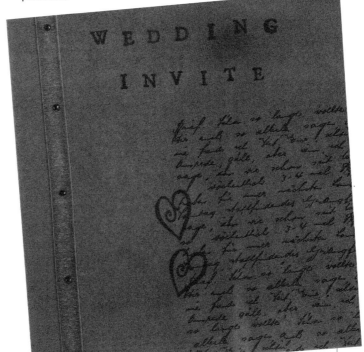

The Complete Cardmaking Handbook

Fluffy Heart
by Cath Allen

Materials:
- ☐ gold-coloured card
- ☐ chocolate brown & burgundy mulberry papers
- ☐ silver paint marker writing pen
- ☐ straight-edged scissors
- ☐ small paintbrush
- ☐ cup of water
- ☐ double-sided tape
- ☐ brown ribbon
- ☐ A4 white paper

To create:

1 Draw a heart shape onto the chocolate brown mulberry paper with the silver paint marker, then a slightly smaller heart shape on the burgundy mulberry paper.

2 Using the paintbrush, wet around the edges of the drawn hearts, following the silver line. Tear along the wet line to get a rough torn-edge effect. Make sure all the silver pen mark is removed.

3 Place double-sided tape onto both hearts, sticking the brown one onto the gold card and the smaller burgundy one onto the brown heart.

4 Type 'wedding invitation' on your computer and print onto the A4 white paper. Cut out the wording as small as you can and stick onto a strip of the ribbon with double-sided tape. Then attach it to the invite.

Turquoise Circles
by Cath Allen

Materials:
- ☐ white card
- ☐ white and silver fleck card
- ☐ silver card
- ☐ peel-offs
- ☐ turquoise hologram circle paper
- ☐ metal confetti (champagne glasses & stars)
- ☐ silver marker

To create:

1 Score and fold the white card, cut to size the white and silver fleck card and adhere to the left-hand side of the base card. Do the same with the silver card using double-sided sticky tape. Stick a peel-off strip down securely along the join.

2 Cut to size a piece of the turquoise hologram paper, then from this cut a smaller square by measuring approx 1.5cm from the edges and cutting this out using the craft knife. Cut out an acetate square and attach to the turquoise hologram frame using double-sided tape. Put the frame upside down on your table and adhere double-sided foam to the back of the acetate, ensuring there are no gaps, and press down firmly.

3 Place metal confetti in a small neat pile onto the main card, and stick the turquoise frame to the card, pressing firmly. Cut to size a piece of the white and silver fleck card. Pencil rule a line, write 'Wedding' in silver, let it dry and rub out the pencil line.

4 Using the smaller peel-off strips, stick these round the edges of the turquoise frame and the 'Wedding' card. Attach the wording to the bottom right-hand corner of the main card with double-sided foam.

Pink Stripe Invite
by Cath Allen

Materials:
- [ ] pink cardstock
- [ ] yellow felt paper
- [ ] orange fabric sunflowers
- [ ] various buttons
- [ ] Hero Arts Heart stamp
- [ ] red fibre
- [ ] I kan'dee Cherish charm
- [ ] striped pink card
- [ ] Wedding Invitation WW 1171E stamp
- [ ] Anita's All Purpose Glue
- [ ] double-sided tape

To create:

1 Using the example as a guide, fold the cardstock in half. Stick the striped pink card to the main card using double-sided tape.

2 Cut two strips of the yellow felt paper and stamp 'Wedding Invitation' down them. Stick these onto the card.

3 Glue the buttons to the centre of the flowers and stick them onto the card.

4 Stamp the heart stamp around the flowers, attach the Cherish charm to the red fibre and tie around the spine of the card.

Purple Hearts
by Cath Allen

Materials:
- [ ] white cardstock
- [ ] Handmade Paper Company purple hearts
- [ ] Deluxe Designs Natural deluxe chalks

To create:

1 Stick the left-hand heart down with double-sided tape, then affix the right-hand one with a small piece of double-sided foam.

2 Using the eye-shadow applicator, touch chalk around the edges of the card.

3 Type 'on your wedding' and cut out the wording.

4 To finish, stick the wording onto the card using double-sided foam.

CHRISTMAS

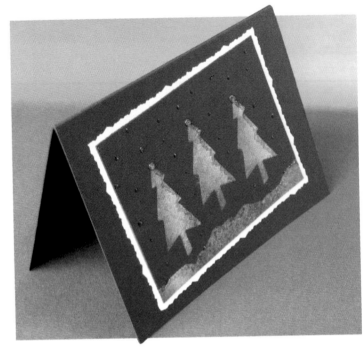

Green Tree
by Dyan Reaveley

Materials:
- □ green card & white card
- □ scrap paper
- □ Iridescent Appliglue
- □ EK Success Tree punch
- □ Moonlight White Brilliance inkpad
- □ stipple brush
- □ deckle-edged scissors
- □ repositionable glue

To create:

1 Cut green card to A5 and fold to make the base card.

2 Punch three tree shapes into scrap paper and tear along the bottom edge to create a mask. Using repositional glue, attach the mask to a piece of card.

3 Stipple through the tree shapes and torn-edge bottom with Moonlight White ink. Remove mask.

4 Trim card to size and attach to a white piece of card. Trim the edges with deckle-edged scissors. Attach at an angle to the folded green card.

5 Decorate trees and sky with Iridescent Appliglue.

Snowman
by Dyan Reaveley

Materials:
- □ white card
- □ JudiKins Frame 2717G, Snowman 2715G & Merry Christmas 6731I stamps
- □ Hero Arts Holiday Script H3164 stamp
- □ Ancient Page Palm Leaf, Coral Red & Lapis Blue inkpads
- □ Karisma green, red, blue & orange pencils
- □ scalpel
- □ cutting mat
- □ Post-it notes

To create:

1 Cut a piece of card to measure 14.5x29cm and fold it in half.

2 Stamp the frame stamp in the upper half of the card using the Palm Leaf inkpad.

3 Place Post-it notes all around the frame, leaving a square free in the middle. Ink the Snowman stamp with Lapis Blue and stamp into the square. Remove Post-its.

4 Place the cutting mat into the card and, using a sharp scalpel, cut inside the frame, leaving the snowman attached.

5 Colour the frame and snowman with Karisma pencils. Ink the Merry Christmas stamp with Palm Leaf and stamp underneath the frame.

6 Open the card, ink the Holiday Script with Coral Red and stamp centrally inside the card. Ensure that you can see the greeting behind the snowman when the card is closed.

Materials:

- ☐ silver pearlescent card
- ☐ Paper Adventures Winter Paper Mix patterned paper
- ☐ silver snowflake confetti
- ☐ silver peel-off greeting
- ☐ silver inkpad
- ☐ 3D foam pads

Snowflakes & Stars
by Natalie O'Shea

To create:

1. Cut an 11cm square from the snowflake patterned paper. Mark out a star design on the back (or use a template if you have one), and cut the aperture using a craft knife.

2. Cut a 10.5cm square of acetate and stick it to the back of the snowflake-patterned paper.

3. Attach 3D foam pads or tape close to the outside edges of the star aperture. Put the snowflake paper face down, pour in your confetti and remove the backing of the sticky fixers/tape. Removing the tape after placing the confetti will ensure that the confetti does not stick to the surface.

4. Cut a 10.5cm square of silver card and place over the sticky fixers/tape. There's your shaker box. All the confetti should be contained within the aperture and sealed tightly. Run a silver inkpad around the edges of the patterned paper. Attach four of the snowflake confetti to the corners of the patterned paper.

5. Cut a 12.5cm square of light blue card and run a silver inkpad around the edge. Attach the shaker box to the centre. Cut a 13cm square of dark blue card and attach the shaker box to the centre. Cut a 13.5cm square of snowflake patterned paper and attach the shaker box to the centre. Then secure to the top of your silver card.

6. Attach the silver peel-off greeting to a piece of light blue card. Ink the edges as before. Using 3D foam pads, stick this to a piece of snowflake-patterned paper, leaving a small border, and ink the edges of this paper with your silver inkpad. Finally, attach this to a dark blue piece of card so that you have a small, even border and attach this centrally under your shaker box.

Santas
by Dyan Reaveley

Materials:

- ☐ white card, red card & black card
- ☐ Creative Stamping Santa hh456e stamp
- ☐ Hero Arts Holiday Script h3164 stamp
- ☐ wet-look embossing markers – primary set
- ☐ Rocket Red Brilliance inkpad
- ☐ clear embossing powder
- ☐ heat gun
- ☐ Iridescent Appliglue
- ☐ Ancient Page Coal inkpad
- ☐ Making Memories metal star shape
- ☐ red eyelet
- ☐ hole punch
- ☐ eyelet setter
- ☐ hammer

To create:

1. Cut white card to 21cm squared. Fold and set aside. Cut a piece of white card to 12x6cm. Ink the Santa stamp with Coal ink and stamp onto the bottom of the card.

2. Stamp the image onto scrap paper three times and cut it out. (These are your masks so cut carefully!) Place one mask on the stamped Santa image and stamp another Santa either side. Place masks over all three Santas.

3. Ink up the Holiday Script stamp with Rocket Red and stamp above the Santas. Remove masks. Colour Santas with embossing markers and clear powder. Heat to set.

4. Cut the edges of the card into a tag shape and mount onto red then black card. Punch a hole in the tag and attach the metal star with a red eyelet. Attach the tag to the card.

5. Add iridescent Appliglue to the fur and beard of the middle Santa.

6. Using red marker, ink up the Merry Christmas part of the Holiday Script stamp and apply to the bottom of the card.

Glittery Tree
by Natalie O'Shea

Materials:
- Art Institute Dries White glue & green glitter
- green mulberry paper
- gold pearlescent card
- green Funky Foam
- gold metallic rub-ons
- Creative Stamping Tree LL357H stamp

To create:

1 Cut a piece of green Funky Foam big enough to stamp your image into. Heat the foam (make sure an adult does this!). Whilst still hot, press the stamp into the Funky Foam and leave for a few seconds to cool. Gently lift your stamp and you will be left with an impression of the image debossed into the foam.

2 Cut a triangle around the stamped image and rub metallic rub-ons all over the foam. This will make the image and words stand out.

3 Mount your triangle onto another piece of green Funky Foam, leaving a small border. Mount this again onto gold pearlescent card.

4 Mount the gold card onto green mulberry paper. Put a paintbrush or cotton bud into water and gently draw round the triangle. Tease the paper apart at the watermark to achieve the feathered edge. It is a lot easier to tear when wet than when dry. Attach this matted triangle onto the centre of your card.

5 Dot blobs of Art Institute glue randomly all over the background of your card. Sprinkle over the glitter, shake vigorously and leave to dry.

Christmas Gifts
by Dyan Reaveley

Materials:
- white card
- Françoise Collection Black Present peel-off
- Rocket Red Brilliance inkpad
- stipple brush
- Happy Christmas peel-off

To create:

1 Cut white card to A5 size and fold. Take two present peel-offs and place near the top of the card.

2 Stipple over the peel-offs using the brush and the red ink. Remove the peel-offs and position further down the card. Stipple with red ink.

3 Repeat until the card is covered and attach the Happy Christmas greeting to finish.

Happy Holidays
by Dyan Reaveley

Materials:
- ☐ cream card, white card & red card
- ☐ scrap paper
- ☐ Woodware Tag punch
- ☐ Hero Arts Holiday Trees C2866 stamp
- ☐ Rocket Red Brilliance inkpad
- ☐ hole punch
- ☐ eyelet setter
- ☐ hammer
- ☐ red eyelet
- ☐ Karisma red & green pencils

To create:

1 Cut a piece of white card to 12x24cm. Fold in half and put it to one side.

2 Punch a tag shape from scrap paper to make a reverse mask.

3 Cut a piece of cream card to 8cm squared. Place the reverse mask over it and stipple Rocket Red ink through tag shape.

4 Ink the Tree stamp with Rocket Red and stamp through the tag shape. Repeat around the edges of the card.

5 Colour the central image with Karisma pencils. Attach to a piece of red card and tear around the edges of the card.

6 Punch a hole at the top of the tag shape and attach a red eyelet. Attach to the folded card.

A Pile of Presents
by Dyan Reaveley

Materials:
- ☐ white card & green card
- ☐ Françoise Collection black peel-off
- ☐ Gamma Green Brilliance inkpad
- ☐ stipple brush
- ☐ Hero Arts Holiday Script H3164 stamp
- ☐ red & green felt tips
- ☐ scrap paper

To create:

1 Cut the white card to A5 size and fold it in half.

2 Tear down the right-hand side of the scrap paper, ensuring that it is big enough to cover the A5 card. Place over the card leaving about an inch showing at the right-hand side.

3 Using the stipple brush, apply Gamma Green ink over the unmasked area. Ink the stamp with Gamma Green and stamp repeatedly down the card. Remove the scrap paper.

4 Stick the Present peel-off onto a piece of white card and colour with felt tips.

5 Trim close to the image and mount onto green card. Place in the top half of the card, using the example as a guide.

6 Colour the greeting stamp with green felt tip, and stamp this in the lower half of the card, under the peel-off image.

Glossary

It sometimes feels like crafters have a secret language, but this really isn't the case. This glossary should help you get to grips with some of the main terms

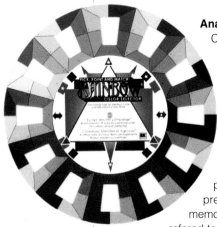

Analogous colours
Colours that lie next to one another on the colour wheel

Aperture
A die-cut opening in the front of a card. It can be a variety of shapes and sizes

Archival
A term used to describe a product or technique used in preserving artefacts, photographs, memorabilia and other items. Normally refered to in scrapbooking

Blending tool
A tool used to blend coloured pencils to create different shades of a colour. Your index finger can be used to do the same job

Brads
These come in all shapes and sizes and resemble paper fasteners

Calligraphy
Formal, old-fashioned lettering

Cardstock
Thick, sturdy paper available in a variety of weights. Normally acid free

Clip art
Artwork in a book or software form with pictures that can be used for cards and scrapbooks

Collage
Artistic compositions created using various materials (paper, cloth, wood etc) that are glued onto a surface

Colour wheel
A wheel that shows colour relationships and placement

Corner punch
A punch that will create a shape or design in the corner of your cards

Corrugated paper
Thick, wavy cardstock available in many colours

Decorative scissors
Scissors that cut in a pattern due to shaped blades, such as deckle-edged scissors (which produce wavy lines)

Die-cuts
Paper designs cut out with a die-cutting machine. Paper is placed on the die and pressure is applied either by rolling or pressing down on the handle

Double-dipped cardstock
A heavyweight quality card that usually has a different colour or pattern on the reverse side. The core is white so it is ideal for tearing

Dry embossing
Dry embossing produces a subtle but sophisticated appearance using a stylus to raise the surface of the paper by burnishing a design through a template. Metal templates work the best, but you may also use the plastic ones designed for stencilling

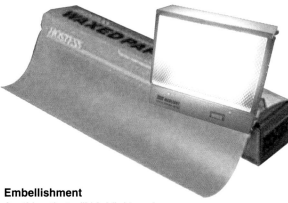

Embellishment
Anything that will highlight and decorate your design: usually charms, fibres, ribbons, tags, stickers, die-cuts, punches etc

Embossing
Creating a raised surface by applying heat or pressure

Eyelets
A small metal ring which is set on the reverse. Used for decorative and setting purposes, they are available in various sizes, colours & shapes

Handmade paper
Often rough and uneven in texture. It is sometimes embedded with flowers and leaves, which add to the natural look

Intaglio
(*in-tal-eo*) A stamping technique that involves pressing something into a receptive surface in order to make an imprint

Iris folding
A technique that originated in Holland. Coloured strips of folded paper are taped into place over a pattern, which creates a spiral design resembling an iris

Lacé
A cutting and folding technique using a specialist metal template and sharp knife. A design is cut in the direction of the arrows on the template using a sharp pointed knife as your tool. You then fold the triangles outwards, pushing them back through the slits

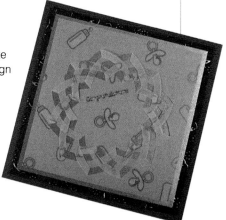

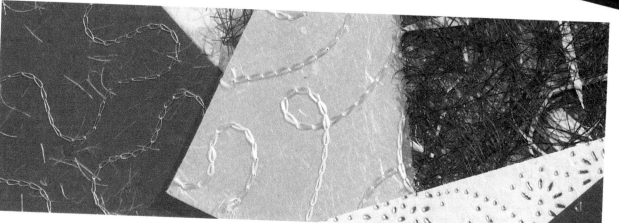

Glossary

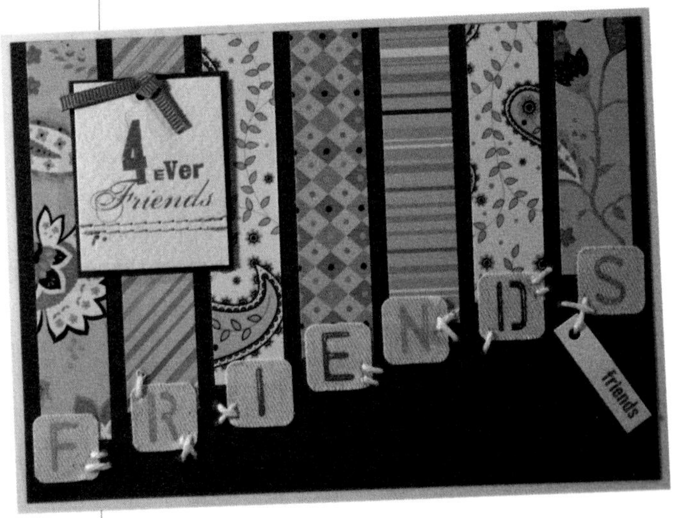

Machine stitching
Made by sewing machines, usually using two threads

Masking
Covering or sectioning off parts of a design with Post-it notes or tape then adding on top of it to give dimension and layers

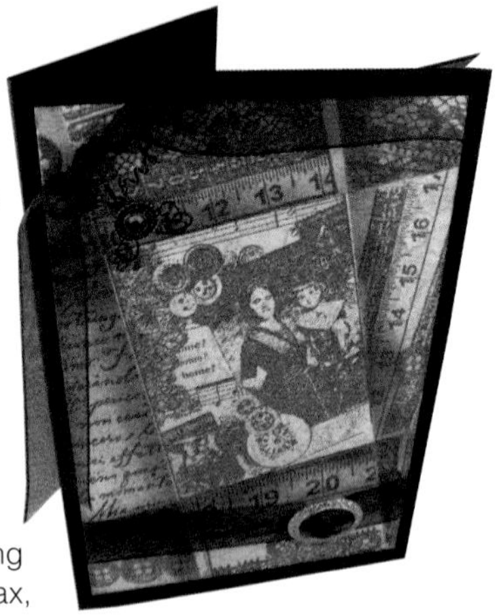

Melting Pot
A non-stick pan that has optimum temperature controls and large handles for pouring and lifting. You can melt, dip and pour UTEE, embossing powders, soap, candle wax, glue, candy and more

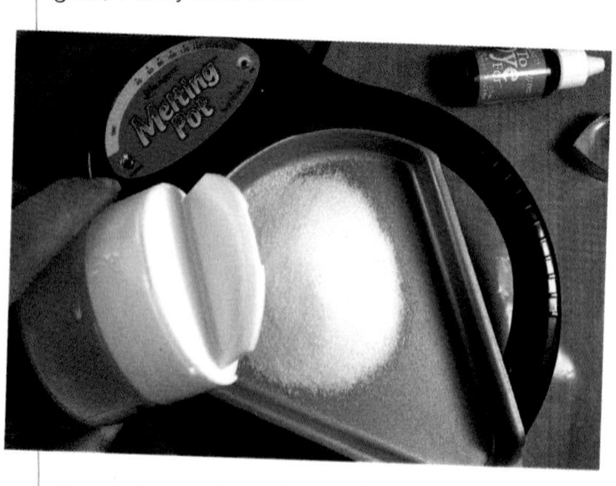

Monochromatic colour scheme
A colour scheme based on different tints and shades of one hue

Muted colours
Tints or shades that tend to be more suitable for backgrounds as they are more subtle

Paint pens
Pens with soft, brush-like tips. The amount of ink dispensed is controlled by the pressure that is applied to the tip. They are often metallic

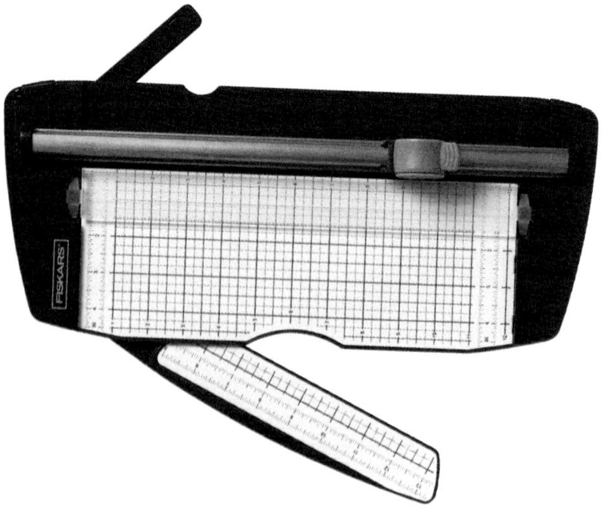

Paper trimmers
Paper-cutting tools used by lining paper up on a grid and moving a blade down or across. Also known a a guillotine

Peel-offs
Special craft stickers that are often holographic

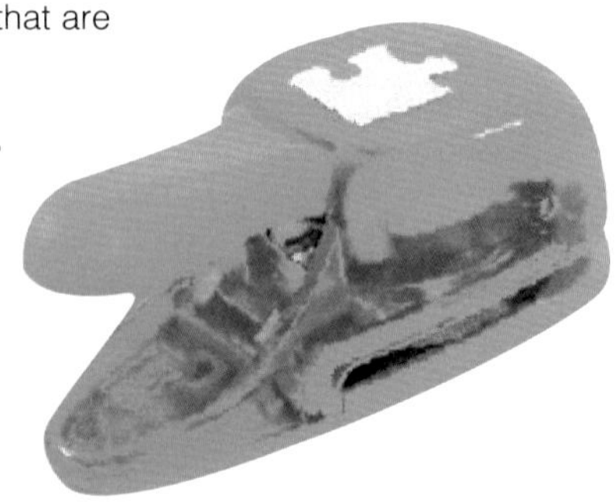

Pre-embossed paper
Paper with a raised design, available as vellum and cardstock

Punch
A tool used to create small shapes by punching them out of paper or card

Punchies
The shapes created by a punch

Quilling
The art of creating decorative designs from thin strips of curled paper. Using simple tools, long strips of paper are tightly wound, released then tweaked to form complex shapes

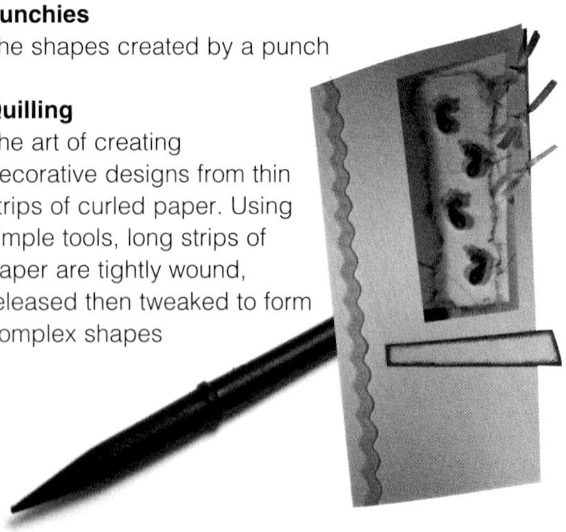

Rubberstamp
A detailed, intricate design cut out of rubber and mounted on wood or foam, or alternatively unmounted (allowing you to store them more easily)

Rub-ons
Craft transfers that are applied by rubbing the design or words onto paper or card with a lolly stick or applicator tool

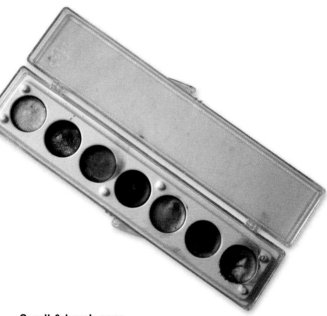

Scroll & brush pens
Pens that have one tip for colouring or blending and one for writing

Secondary colours
Colours created by blending two primary colours. Orange, green and violet are the secondary colours created by mixing a combination of red, yellow and blue

Shade
A colour that has had black mixed into it

Snap
A type of eyelet but without the hole in the middle

Stitching
The process of attaching a number of mediums together, or adding a pattern, using a needle and thread or fibres

Template
A stencil or design that can be traced, allowing your to create elements for your design

Tertiary colours
Blends of primary and secondary colours, such as red-orange and blue-green

Tint
A colour that has had white mixed into it

UTEE
Ultra Thick Embossing Enamel is a specially formulated, large-particle embossing powder. It can be used in the same way as ordinary embossing powders or can be used in melt art

Vellum
A lightweight, translucent paper that looks like tracing paper, but comes in all different colours and thicknesses. Great for embossing on

Watercolour
A painting technique making use of water-soluble pigments that are either transparent or opaque and are formulated to bond the pigment to the paper

Xyron
A machine that applies adhesive to pages and can also laminate

Templates

Here are some handy templates to use as directed in the relevant project steps on the previous pages, along with a couple of cardmakers' favourites

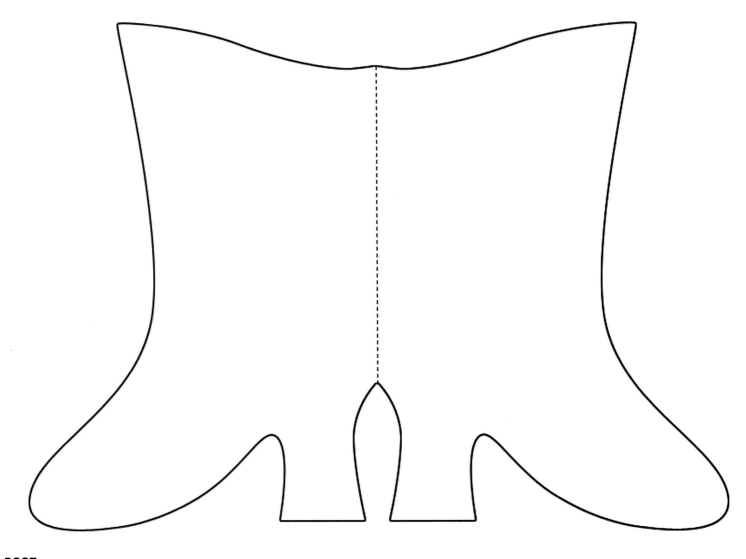

BOOT
p101
Not to scale

Start here

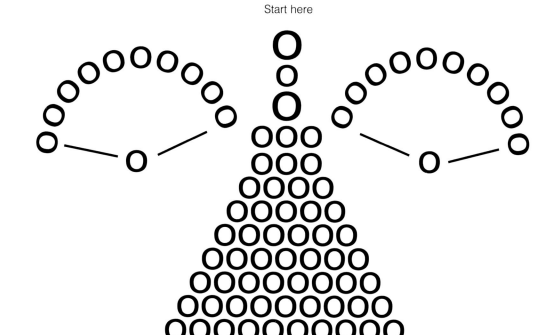

ANGEL
p28

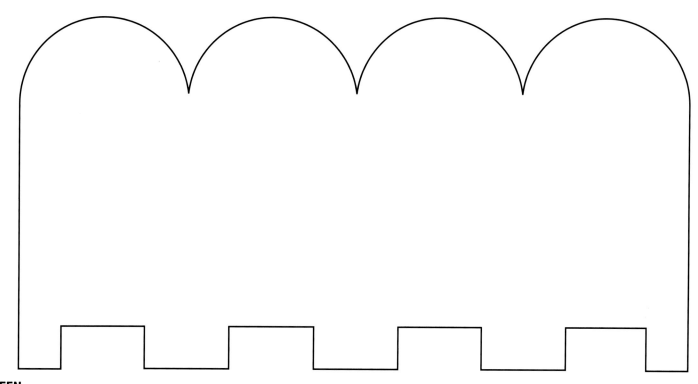

SCREEN
p22

Folding

Metal & Wire

Haberdashery

Altered

Celebrate

Seasonal

Theory

Stick & Quick

Punch Art

Embossing

Stamping

UTEE

Plastics

FLOWER
p74

TAG

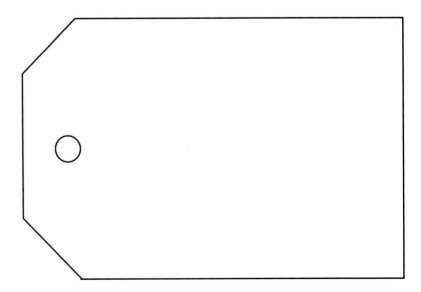

IRIS FOLDING
p95

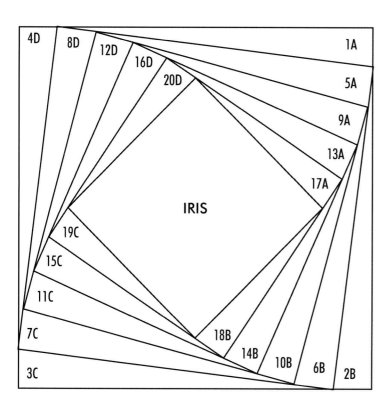

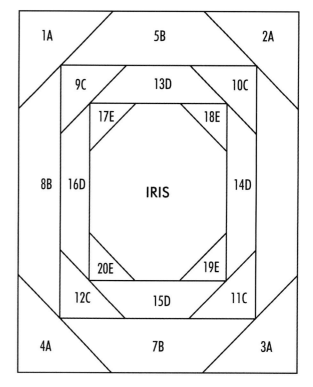

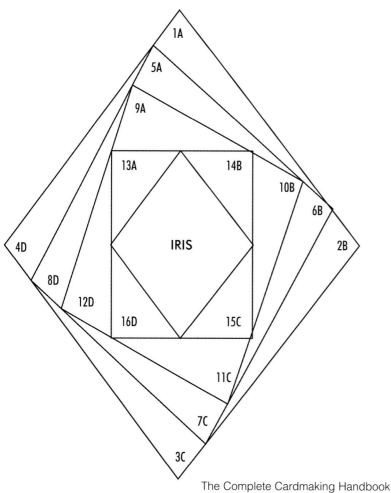

Folding

Metal & Wire

Haberdashery

Altered

Celebrate

Seasonal

GIFT BOX

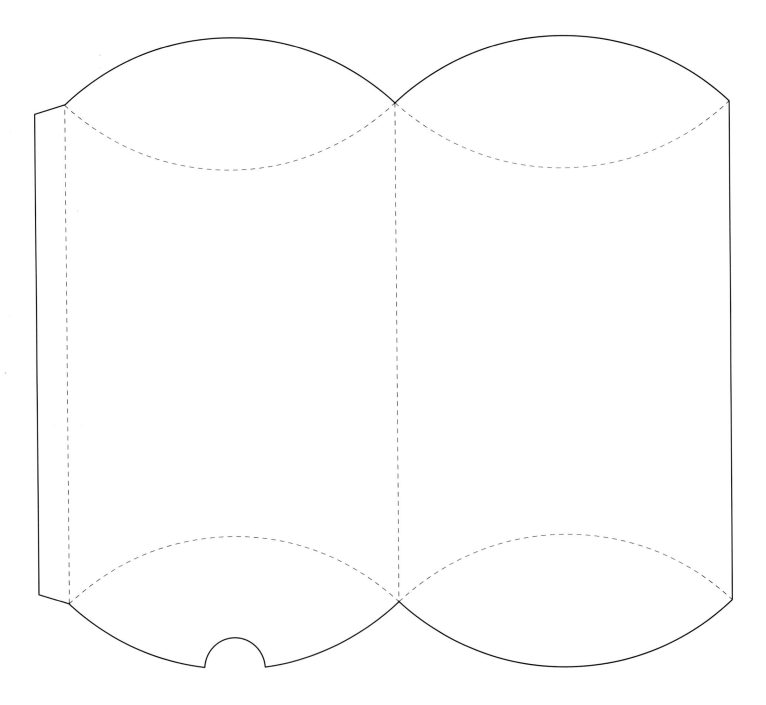

The Complete Cardmaking Handbook

GIFT BAG

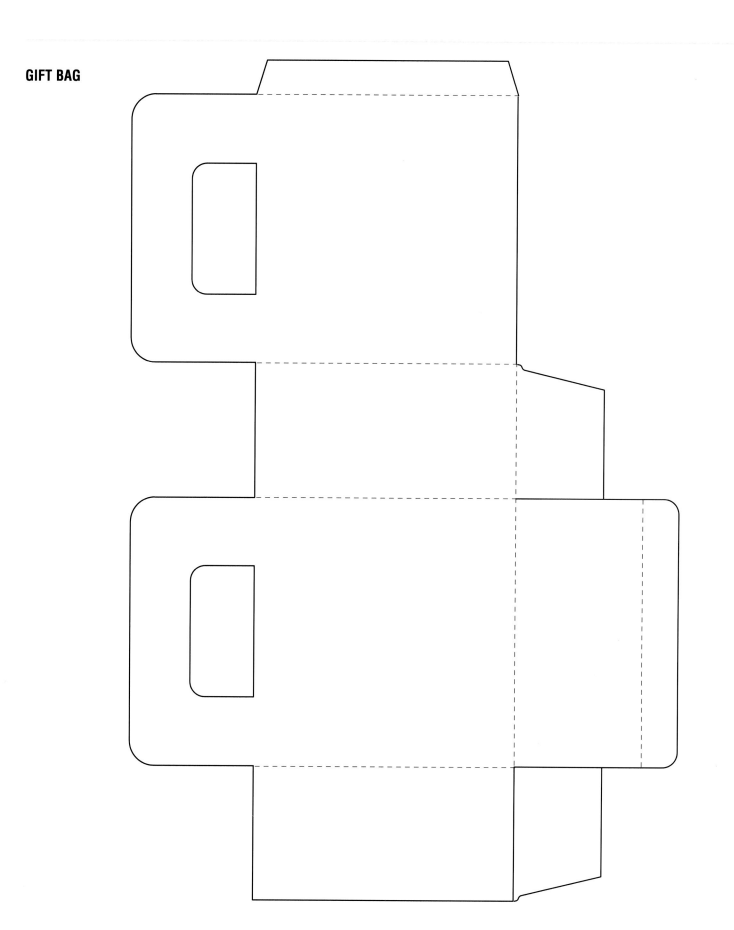

Folding

Metal & Wire

Haberdashery

Altered

Celebrate

Seasonal

Supplies Guide

*Here are just some of the many manufacturers of craft products
who make and sell items featured in this handbook*

Beads

Provo Craft
www.provocraft.com
Distributor: Bramwells Yarns & Crafts
www.bramwellcrafts.co.uk
01282 860 388

Chalks

Pebbles Inc. I kan'dee
www.pebblesinc.com
Distributor: ScrapGenie Ltd
www.scrapgenie.com
01440 704 400

EK Success
www.eksuccess.com
Distributor: Bramwells Yarns & Crafts
www.bramwellcrafts.co.uk
01282 860 388

Die-cutting Machines

Sizzix
www.sizzix.com
Distributor: Ellison www.sizzix.com
08706 000 625

QuicKutz
www.quickutz.com
Distributor: Personal Impressions
www.richstamp.co.uk
01787 375 241

Craft Robo
www.graphtecgb.com
01978 666 700

Zip'eMate
www.zipemate.com
Distributor: Kars & Co BV
www.kars.biz
+31(0) 344 642 864

Embossing Stencils

Lasting Impressions
www.lastingimpressions.com
Distributor: ScrapGenie Ltd
www.scrapgenie.com
01440 704 400

American Traditional Designs
www.americantraditional.com
Distributor: Personal Impressions
www.richstamp.co.uk
01787 375 241

Haberdashery

Junkitz
www.junkitz.com
Distributor: Scrapbook Trade
www.scrapbooktrade.co.uk
01505 871 332

Chatterbox
www.chatterboxinc.com
Distributor: ScrapGenie Ltd
www.scrapgenie.com
01440 704 400

sei
www.shopsei.com
Distributor: Scrapbook Trade
www.scrapbooktrade.co.uk
01505 871 332

Buttons Galore
www.buttonsgalore.com
Distributor: Bramwells Yarns & Crafts
www.bramwellcrafts.co.uk
01282 860 388

American Crafts
www.americancrafts.com
Distributor: thescrapbookhouse
www.thescrapbookhouse.com
0870 770 7717

Coats Crafts UK

www.coatscrafts.co.uk
01325 394 237

Heat Embossing Tools

Heat It Up! tool
Distributor: Do Crafts
www.docrafts.co.uk
01202 811 000

Heat It craft tool
www.rangerink.com
Distributor: Personal Impressions
www.richstamp.co.uk
01787 375 241

Inks/Dies/Stains

Whispers
Distributor: Do Crafts
www.docrafts.co.uk
01202 811 000

Ranger Industries
www.rangerink.com
Distributor: Personal Impressions
www.richstamp.co.uk
01787 375 241

ColorBox
www.clearsnap.com
Distributor: Woodware Craft Collection
01756 700 024

Lacé

Lacé Templates
Distributor: Kars & Co BV
www.kars.biz+31(0) 344 642 864

American Traditional Designs
www.americantraditional.com
Distributor: Personal Impressions
www.richstamp.co.uk
01787 375 241

The Complete Cardmaking Handbook

Index

Index

Folding

Metal & Wire

Haberdashery

Altered

Celebrate

Seasonal